*Keep
mike*

WIND

THE TRIED AND TRUE

RECESSION BUSTING

NATION CHANGING

JOB PRODUCING

REVIVAL CAUSING

SOLUTION TO CONTEMPORARY

ECONOMIC AND CULTURAL

PROBLEMS

Dedication

This little book is dedicated to Bea, my mother-in-law.
Bea is one of the three most inspirational women
I have ever known.
I am fortunate enough to have been married
to one of the other two for over forty years.

. . . and thanks

I would like to express my gratitude to Lesley.
She spent countless hours ferreting out
and correcting my mistakes.
Undoubtedly there remain some errors in this book,
but only because I revisited some pages
after she was finished. Thanks Lesley.

WIND

THE TRIED AND TRUE
RECESSION BUSTING
NATION CHANGING
JOB PRODUCING
REVIVAL CAUSING
SOLUTION TO CONTEMPORARY
ECONOMIC AND CULTURAL
PROBLEMS

MIKE CARRIER

ALISTAIR RAPIDS PUBLISHING INC.

GRAND RAPIDS, MICHIGAN

Wind

Wind—The Tried and True Recession Busting Nation Changing Job Producing Revival Causing Solution to Contemporary Economic and Cultural Problems. Copyright 2009 by Mike Carrier.

Published 2009 by Alistair Rapids Publishing, Grand Rapids, MI.

All Scripture quoted is taken from the NEW AMERICAN STANDARD BIBLE®, Copyright © 1960, 1962, 1963, 1968, 1971, 1972, 1973, 1975, 1977, 1995 by The Lockman Foundation. Used by permission.

All quotes attributed to AGCEQ are from *America's God and Country Encyclopedia of Quotations,* published by FAME Publishing, Coppell, TX, 1994.

Visit the website at www.newrevivalist.com. For upcoming books by the same author visit www.alistairpublishing.com. The cover was designed by Evie Carrier, using an image purchased from Istock.com.

ISBN: 978-1-936092-38-3 (trade pbk)
Printed in the United States of America

Library of Congress Cataloging-in-Publication Data

Carrier, Mike.
Wind—The Tried and True Recession Busting Nation Changing Job Producing Revival Causing Solution to Contemporary Economic and Cultural Problems / by Mike Carrier. 1st ed.
Includes bibliography.
ISBN: 978-1-936092-38-3 (trade pbk. : alk. paper)
1. Revival 2. Recession Busting 3. Inflation Chasing 4. Nation Changing 5. Job Producing 6. Clarion Call 7. Solution to Economic and Cultural Problems.

Contents

Notes from the author

This book has been called simplistic. I prefer to think of it as *uncomplicated*; but I don't object to either description. I have found that most often in life it is the simple thing that confounds the complex.

I am not alone in my adoration of simplicity. Albert Einstein rethought his work constantly, always seeking lowest common denominators. I would bet that when a generally accepted unified theory emerges from the mind of the next Einstein (or super computer), it will be sufficiently concise to fit on a postage stamp.

When reading *Wind* chapters involving U.S. history, I would encourage readers not to assume that just because the facts included in those sections might not align themselves with the schema of history they have learned, that my facts are bogus.

The problem is that most people have developed their notion of U.S. history from high school textbooks, not realizing that all such books are to one degree or another products of interpretation, with most being *seriously* skewed.

If a reader questions what I have written (particularly regarding history), he should research it for himself. It is important, however, that this research be done using only primary and sound secondary sources—*no* textbooks. Doctoral dissertations written by PhD candidates at quality universities (those known for research—*never* schools of education) are usually helpful in this, as they are at least generally based on appropriate source material.

An amazing amount of information can be accessed online; but I have learned never to assume that what I find there is correct.

One of the early criticisms I fielded had to do with *Wind's* subtitle.

Some thought it to be not only inordinately long, but misleading as well. I accept the observation that the subtitle is long (perhaps even too long); but I take exception to the thought that it is not accurate. I wholeheartedly believe that national revival will lay the groundwork for the sort of economic engine that produces prosperity; and that national revival is the *only* way to solve our cultural problems.

Another criticism of *Wind* relates to the authoritative posture I assumed in its writing. It has even been suggested that I intend to portray *Wind* as something akin to an "inspired" work. Trust me when I assure readers that I do not think *Wind* was inspired. While I do have a lot of confidence in the veracity of what I have included between these covers, I do not for a moment claim divine inspiration. (Besides, had God written *Wind,* He would not have felt constrained to put a bibliography at the end; nor would He have needed Lesley to proofread it so many times.)

I anticipate the disregard (if not disdain) with which this book will be greeted by all but the most open-minded of secularists. I can't say that pleases me, but there is little I can do about it.

The only encouragement I can offer here is to suggest that it is always good to expand horizons, and occasionally be forced to rethink the foundations upon which one builds his trust.

Perhaps *Wind* can help in that regard.

Finally, if this book upsets you, please don't email me with your take on all the possible alternative views regarding the topics it covers—assume I'm aware of most of them. If, however, you find a typo, grammatical error, misquote, or an inadvertent unattributed quote, please let me know that. I would like to correct those mistakes for future printings.

Comments can be sent to the publisher (Alistair Rapids Publishing, 1029 28th Street SE, Grand Rapids, MI 49508), emailed (revival.wind@gmail.com), or via *Wind's* blog (http://windthebook.wordpress.com).

Preface

Some thinkers have already written America off. For instance, in 2008 Fareed Zakaria wrote a *New York Times* Best Seller entitled *The Post-American World* in which he outlined just such a scenario.

According to many academics and philosophers (such as Mr. Zakaria), America's role as a leader in the world is on the wane. Even some of our current political leaders are looking to the rest of the world for guidance through our tough times. They are speaking as though America's best days are long gone.

Well, perhaps they are right. Maybe it is time to give up and bow down to what the world wants us to do; to surrender our liberties, and our leadership. Perhaps it is time for capitulation.

But, we do have a choice. And the choice is clear and real. In earlier times, when faced with similar circumstances, America (and other God-centric countries) simply heeded the imperative stated in the Old Testament: "If . . . My people who are called by My name humble themselves and pray and seek My face and turn from their wicked ways, then I will hear from heaven, will forgive their sin and will heal their land" (2 Chron. 7:13-14).

Nothing could be more clear, or more simple. Within that short statement resides all that is required of us to find our way back. It has worked before, and it will work again.

This book explains in clear terminology how you can do your part to help bring about the restoration of our country through a Third Great Awakening.

Wind is a call for national revival—a clarion call.

Cursed be all learning that is contrary to the cross of Christ.

—Jonathan Dickinson, first president of Princeton.

Introduction

During a four-year period of time, dating from 1993 through 1997, I spent all day every Tuesday in fasting and prayer. Because I found it very difficult to concentrate around my house or office, I would jump in my car and drive approximately ninety miles to a sixty-foot house trailer my wife and I were buying.

The trailer was located at a campground on Grass Lake, which is located in Eastern Jackson County, Michigan. Fortunately the price of gas at that time was about one dollar per gallon.

I would then spend the day in fasting and prayer, returning home to Grand Rapids in time for dinner.

During the sessions of fasting and prayer, I ate nothing, but I did drink a lot of water and some coffee. I never viewed those days as sacrificial—not in any way. In fact, I considered it a privilege that I was able to leave my business in the capable hands of some wonderful people. The most capable and wonderful of all, of course, was my wife Evie. Even though my Tuesday absence during those forty-eight months did place added pressure on her (we still had four children at home, and a business to run), she never once complained.

This is what my typical Tuesday looked like. I would get up at my usual time (5 a.m.), go into the office and check my messages, and make any necessary decisions concerning what occurred during the night. My wife and I operated our own security company, and frequently burglars would choose the night-time to perpetrate their dirty deeds.

Once I had determined that the sky was not about to fall without me, I would head out of town. I think it is significant that during those four years, there was not a single incident that took place that prevented my going to the trailer, nor did I experience any ill health. I was always able to kiss Evie goodbye, and head toward Jackson, before any of our day shift employees arrived (which was at 8 a.m.).

Once at the trailer, I would read from numerous books (primarily about periods of revival), and from the Bible. And, of course, I would pray.

During every one of those sessions, I would end the day by writing down my thoughts. Sometimes they would be lengthy; sometimes they comprised only a handful of words. I then printed what I wrote in a newsletter I published (*The New Revivalist*).

Approximately two hundred of the articles were then reprinted as a column ("Wind of Revival") in at least a couple of small newspapers.

This book (*Wind*) contains about one-third of the work I did during those four years.

Should demand dictate, *Wind Volume Two* could be released in 2010. If so, it will also contain about one-third of the articles. However, no final decision has been made regarding the publishing of any additional volumes.

There are at least a few dozen articles that I cannot locate (perhaps they will turn up later). Unfortunately, the software I used at the time I originally wrote them is no longer supported. That makes reconstitution very difficult.

One of the more memorable events that occurred during those two hundred Tuesdays actually took place while I was en route to the trailer.

I had found that the best highway to take was I-96. While there were shorter routes, the interstate allowed me hit cruise, and pretty much forget traffic signs.

I-96 took me through the southern outskirts of Lansing (State Capital of Michigan), after which I would catch the Jackson exit.

And, perhaps one of the best things about the interstate was that there were plenty of public restrooms available. Remember, I said I did like to hydrate my body when I fasted.

On one particular trip, I realized that I was going to have to stop at a restroom sooner than usual. I was still about thirty minutes west of Lansing at the time.

I found a convenient rest stop, parked, and rushed into the facility to relieve myself. As I hurried along on the sidewalk, I did notice that a man wearing a suit was standing there as though waiting for someone. He never said a word, and we never made eye contact.

As I made my way back to my car after leaving the facility, I again noticed the man still standing where he was when I entered. Before I got to my car, he turned and said, "Hi, Mike."

I then looked at him, and immediately recognized the man. It was Bill Hardiman. Every Sunday morning I would usher Bill and his wife to their seats at church. In fact, for years Bill was my daughter's youth leader.

Bill's full-time job was as mayor of Kentwood, a suburb of Grand Rapids, Michigan. He was (at the time I encountered him on the interstate) transitioning from local politics to state leadership.

"Bill, what's happening?" I asked.

"I'm having a little car trouble. But a tow truck is on the way."

He made sure that I knew that help was coming, so that he would not impose on me.

"What's wrong with your car?" I inquired.

"Don't know. It just started coughing. I was fortunate that I could get off the highway."

I thought for a moment. Here Bill was, looking like a million dollars. "He must be headed to Lansing for a meeting," I thought.

"Where are you going?"

"I'm supposed to deliver a speech this morning," he replied. He then glanced down at his watch.

"What time are you due there?"

"I'm supposed to speak at ten."

"What time is it now?" I asked.

"It's nine."

"You're not going to make it," I said. "Even if the tow truck got here right now, you wouldn't make it."

"I should be okay."

"You have your cell?" I inquired.

"Yes."

"Hide your key on the tire, or somewhere, call the towing company and tell them where to find it. And let them tow it to wherever you want it towed. I will drop you off in Lansing."

"No, I can't do that."

"Sure you can," I said. "Perhaps it is providential. Things do happen like that."

"You've got things to do. I can't impose on you," Bill protested.

"No problem at all. I'm just headed to my trailer for the day. And Lansing is virtually on the way," I insisted.

He made his call, and off we went. I got him to his engagement with time to spare.

As he was getting out of the car, he offered to pay for my gas.

"No, certainly not," I said. "This was not out of my way at all. And it was good talking to you."

"Then let me pray for you," he said. "Do you or your family have any special needs?"

I thought for a few seconds, and answered. "No, we are all healthy and happy." Just hearing myself say that made me thankful.

But then I remembered something. I *did* have a problem. For the past six weeks red squirrels had riddled my trailer. They had crawled between the ceiling and the roof, and had made nests. In at least six places they had gnawed two-inch holes through the ceiling. I suspect they did that to create air flow.

I had tried mothballs, but that didn't help. It only made the trailer stink like a musty attic.

I then bought three ultrasonic devices that were supposed to drive the squirrels nuts; but they only caused my intruders to scamper around all the more.

Finally, I patched up the holes with quick-drying concrete. The squirrels just made new holes.

"You know, I *do* have a problem. I've got a very aggravating squirrel problem," I told him just as he was about to pray.

He raised his head, and stared into my eyes. "*Squirrel* problems?" He asked. "What sort of squirrel problems?"

I then told him the abbreviated version of the story.

Bill then said something like, "You are certainly a blessed man when the only problem you have is a few squirrels."

He was right.

Well, Bill did pray a blessing on me and my family. And, of course, he did ask God to solve my squirrel problem. He then thanked me again, and briskly walked off.

Frankly, I was skeptical about the efficacy of his prayer. Strange as it might seem, even though I was going to the trailer weekly to fast and pray, I never once had asked God to solve my squirrel problem. "Why would God answer Bill's prayer on my behalf, when I never bothered to pray about it myself?" I wondered.

I did finally arrive at the trailer, howbeit maybe an hour later than usual. But it didn't matter to me. I was not on the clock.

I did not give the squirrel issue a thought, except when I got ready to leave that evening. "I have not heard the squirrels running around today," I thought to myself, "perhaps Bill's prayer worked."

There were still five or six air holes the squirrels had gnawed through my ceiling, but I did not bother to patch them up. Apparently I did not have *that* much confidence in Bill's prayer.

For the next three weeks I never heard another squirrel in the ceiling. Finally, after the fourth week, I patched the holes with light plaster. "No point using a permanent patch," I thought, "that might just make them mad again."

Months then passed, and still no evidence of squirrel activity. Then, one Sunday morning, as I was about to seat Bill in church, I grabbed his arm and told him, "Bill, if this politics thing doesn't work out, you could always be an exterminator."

He looked at me strangely, until I briefly told him the story about the squirrels, and how they never came back.

He chuckled and replied, "God is good, isn't He?"

Chapter 1—America and God

S trange as it might seem, America already stands in covenant relationship with God—it isn't even necessary to create any new document.
We don't have to strike any kind of special bargain. We don't even have
to rewrite our history or founding documents to accommodate it. We,
as a nation, already have a solemn covenant with Almighty God. Truly,
revival is in our hand and is ours to claim!

All we have to do is live up to our end of this *existing* agreement with
God, and He will pour out His Spirit upon us again, and heal our land.

Columbus wrote in his personal diary concerning his American
expedition: "It was the Lord who put it into my mind—I could feel His
hand upon me. . . . There is no question that the inspiration was from
the Holy Spirit. . . . The fact that the Gospel must still be preached to so
many lands in such a short time—this is what convinces me."

As the Mayflower approached the New World, those who were about
to become the first settlers wrote these words: "In the name of God,
Amen. We whose names are underwritten, . . . having undertaken, for
the glory of God, and advancement of the Christian faith, and honor of
our king and country, a voyage to plant the first colony in the Northern
parts of Virginia."

"We came into these parts of America," states the New England
Confederation of 1643, "with one and the same end and aim, namely, to
advance the kingdom of our Lord Jesus Christ, and to enjoy the liberties
of the Gospel in purity with peace."

Churches served many functions for the colonists. Not only did they
provide spiritual leadership, but almost all local government in the colonies was housed exclusively within their walls. The churches also served as

the center of education, and for the dissemination of news throughout the colonies. For instance, when our fledgling government wanted to get the Declaration of Independence into the hands of the people, it sent copies out to the local churches. All thirteen original colonies were founded by ministers of the gospel, for the expressed purpose of "suppression of vice and encouraging of religion (Christianity) and virtue," such as is stated in the New Jersey Charter of 1664.

During these early years, nearly all institutions were founded in the name of God. Documents show that 106 out of the first 108 colleges and universities started out as Christian schools. Harvard, Yale, Rutgers, William and Mary, etc., were all founded as Bible Teaching Schools.

It is a simple fact that the Christian Bible was the principal textbook in all the schools throughout the land. Thomas Jefferson, the alleged father of "Separation of Church and State," himself chose the Bible (the "Jefferson Bible") as the basic reader in the New York Public School System (which was under his leadership). Jefferson wrote that religion is "deemed in other countries incompatible with good government, and yet provided by our experience to be its best support." He also maintained that "the Bible is the cornerstone of liberty; . . . students perusal of the sacred volume will make us better citizens."

Again, when Jefferson was put in charge of organizing the Northwest Territory, he authorized the federal government to hire ministers of the gospel for the expressed purpose of aiding in the settlement of the new territory.

George Washington, and virtually all of our early leaders, when faced with tough challenges, would frequently take the three-block walk from Independence Hall, down the street, to Christ Church. There they would spend hours, and sometimes days, in fasting and prayer. In his first inaugural address, Washington declared: "No people can be bound to acknowledge and adore the Invisible Hand which conducts the affairs of men more than the people of the United States. Every step by which they have advanced to the character of an independent nation seems to have been distinguished by some token of Providential Agency. . . . We ought to be no less persuaded that the propitious smiles of Heaven can never be expected on a nation that disregards the eternal rules of order and right which Heaven itself has ordained."

I would like to see this nation again exercise a little more of George Washington's brand of "Providential Agency."

Contrary to popular secular opinion, only one of our Founding Fathers was truly an espoused "deist." That was James Wilson (Virtually all of the others were to one degree or another professing Christians, with a few pure rationalists, such as Thomas Paine, tossed in the mix.).

So, as you can see, we do not have to make a *new* covenant with God—our Founding Fathers have already forged one. We need only to *revive* it! The Bible says, "If . . . My people who are called by My name humble themselves and pray and seek My face and turn from their wicked ways, then I will hear from heaven, will forgive their sin and will heal their land" (2 Chron. 7:13-14).

Pray for revival! Better yet, *earnestly* seek God's face for revival. That's how we hold up our end of our already-existing covenant; that's how we stop the slide, and regain our status as a "blessed nation."

Accept the challenge—pray for national revival, now!

Author's Notes: Even Deist James Wilson did not start out that way. Initially Wilson had studied theology in college aspiring to the Presbyterian ministry. But he had to withdraw due to lack of finances. Unfortunately, Wilson's financial woes did not end when he left college. Throughout his life he exhibited poor financial judgment, having to move from place to place to avoid debtors' prison. That humiliation prevented his internment with other Founding Fathers at Christ Church until long after his death.

*Religion [is] the basis
and Foundation of Government.*

—James Madison, Fourth President of the

United States

and "Chief Architect of the Constitution" (AGCEQ).

Chapter 2—Remember the great 1789 ***British*** *Revolution?*

A good example of revival power can be seen in the great British Revolution of 1789. Do you recall reading about *that* revolution in your World History textbook?

If you don't remember the British Revolution, don't think less of yourself. The truth is, there was no British Revolution in 1789. But there could have been. Similar social and economic conditions existed in both Great Britain and France at that time. While those conditions produced a vicious war in France, England reacted differently to them.

The reason for the difference was revival. At the end of the eighteenth century Great Britain had a huge national revival. France did not. Many historians acknowledge that this great revival saved Great Britain from a bloody upheaval similar to that suffered by its neighbor.

America could learn a lesson from this. Whether we like to think about it or not, America is on the verge of a revolution.

Today, if we were to attempt to pay off our national debt, we would have to sell the entire country to someone with very deep pockets—that simply will not happen. Plus, that debt is only a part of the larger problem. There are over fifty trillion dollars in unfunded liabilities staring us in the face. And it increases daily. There are not enough government programs to terminate to even put a dent in it. Our Government and our institutions have failed us miserably. Historically, when this happens, people revolt.

Could revolution happen in America?

Yes! In fact, it did happen here only two and a half lifetimes ago.

We have no choice. We must have revival—revival instead of revolution. We must do 2 Chronicles 7:14. And we must do it *now*.

The owner of the company had been out of town for a long time. The operation of the business certainly reflected it—production, profits and morale were all down.

"Boy, am I ready for the boss to come back!" Exclaimed the office manager.

"Me too," chimed in the secretary, "I will be very glad to see him."

It was 2 p.m. on Friday, and all the machine operators, truck drivers and design engineers were sitting around the office chewing the fat, and commenting on how much each one of them missed the boss.

Mostly, though, they just watched the time clock.

No steam was coming out of the chimney, no product was flowing off the conveyor belt, no shavings were to be found beneath their drill presses. In general, nothing was happening!

All the tools that the boss had bought for them were neatly hung on the wall.

All the capital that the boss had invested was dormant and declining.

"Boy, I sure hope the boss gets back soon," one worker finally said, ". . . I'll bet he will be happy to see us!"

—The New Revivalist, 1994.

Chapter 3—A new wind

I believe that there is a new wind of revival blowing our way. It has been brought about, at least in part, by the mighty wind of the revival that is sweeping the rest of the world. It has already blown across South America, Eastern Europe, and into Asia. It is reported that there may now be upwards of two hundred million "Secret Christians" in Mainland China alone! In the city of Seoul, South Korea, one single church serves over eight hundred thousand worshippers! Revival meetings in Buenos Aires, Argentina, have drawn crowds estimated at two hundred thousand.

In Brazil, the Christian "born-again" rate is increasing faster than that nation's birth rate. The Bible says that in the end times God would pour out His Spirit on "all mankind; and your sons and daughters will prophesy, your old men will dream dreams, your young men will see visions" (Joel 2:28). Perhaps this is that last great wave of revival!

Possibly the most amazing news of all is how the Spirit of God moved across the old Soviet Union. During the 1990s, public school students there were allowed to receive copies of the Bible as fast as they could be printed—all with the Government's tacit approval, if not outright blessing!

In more recent times there has been a crack down on Bible distribution in Russia, but I doubt that many of the Bibles already in the hands of the public could have been collected and destroyed.

Imagine that: the Russian Government allowed Bibles to be placed in the hands of students, while our Government handed out condoms. How ironic.

America, the cradle of Christianity for the past two hundred years, must prepare herself for this revival. The Bible says, "If . . . My people who are called by My name humble themselves and pray and seek My face and turn from their wicked ways, then I will hear from heaven, and will forgive their sin and will heal their land" (2 Chron. 7:13-14). We must get on our faces before God, now. Or we will miss this revival, and the blessing of God will be withdrawn from us (Rev. 2:1-5).

I am convinced that if we allow this to happen—if we allow this fresh wind of revival to pass us by—our nation will collapse. America needs God's healing touch more now than ever. We must be sensitive to this move of God. We must get rid of pride, and humble ourselves before Him. We must confess our sin, and live righteously. There is no time to waste.

National revival is America's only hope. Let's jump into this new wind of revival, and breathe deeply!

Accept the challenge—pray for national revival, now!

Chapter 4—Chuck

(This account was paraphrased largely from a book edited by Garth M. Rosell and Richard A.G. Dupuis, *The Memoirs of Charles G. Finney*. Grand Rapids: Zondervan Publishing House (1989) pp. 13ff. Additional suggested reading on Charles Finney at end of this chapter.)

Those simple, insignificant, little prayer meetings—what can they *possibly* amount to?

Nothing would ever come of *those* prayer meetings. At least that's what most people in Adams (New York) thought. Not that many people attended the meetings in the first place. Even the pastor of the church, the Rev. Gale, did not have much confidence in them—he didn't attend them either.

Yet, that little band of intercessors remained undaunted. They kept meeting for prayer, week after week, and month after month. They stayed on their faces before God, seeking for revival in their little town.

When they approached Chuck, their young choir director (who also served as the town's practicing attorney) to invite him to their prayer meetings, he just laughed at them.

"How long have you been praying for revival?" Chuck asked.

"Oh, I think it's been a year. . . . Perhaps more for some of us," replied one of the devout.

"And do you have revival?" Chuck queried, in a lawyerly fashion.

"Not yet," was the reply.

"Then why should I pray with you? It is obvious that God does not answer *your* prayers. You are wasting your time. Why should I waste mine?" Chuck retorted.

Nevertheless, that little group of intercessors persisted. They continued to pray for revival. And they prayed specifically for Chuck, who, even while serving as choir director, had come to be known as a "very wicked man."

Then, after nearly another year had passed, God answered the prayers of the intercessors. He sent powerful Holy Spirit conviction upon Chuck. The young man became so miserable because of his sin that he began to hate life itself.

Finally, after resisting as long as he could, Chuck ran out into a secluded forest, promising himself that he would either die there in the woods, or he would be forgiven of his sins.

Nearly a day later Chuck emerged from the forest, cleansed from head to toe. He was a new man. He was "born again."

The funny thing about it was that the intercessors at that humble little church would not believe him. They thought he was putting them on. The pastor wouldn't believe him either. Rev. Gale was convinced that Chuck would remain a pagan forever.

Chuck, however, knew he was sincere. He asked permission to address the entire congregation during the following Sunday service. Rev. Gale reluctantly agreed. Not knowing what to expect, the pastor sat on the edge of his seat, ready to show Chuck his seat, should the situation get out of hand. Chuck did address the congregation that Sunday, and the entire congregation (the Rev. Gale included) was awestruck.

And so began the ministry of Charles (Chuck) Grandison Finney, the most powerful revivalist of the Second Great American Awakening.

Charles Finney is living evidence that there is something special and powerful about intercessory prayer meetings. There is a dynamic in them that defies explanation.

Leaders, don't concern yourselves about what people will think. Don't worry whether anyone will come or not. Just open up your churches for weekly, congregational prayer meetings. It is best to have them in the evenings (preferably Fridays), so working people can participate.

And don't give up right away. If there seems to be a lack of interest and success, just remember—God is looking for obedience, not results. After all, only He can answer prayer anyway.

It's simple—you supply the obedience, He supplies the results.

If you just do this simple, little thing, God will awaken and purify His people. He will send revival to you.

Always remember, while programs and performances may be acceptable *evangelistic* tools, only prayer meetings facilitate revival.

Perhaps there is another Charles Finney sitting in your congregation. Perhaps *you* are that second Charles Finney.

Seek God's face. If you do, He will reveal to you exactly what your role will be in the upcoming revival.

Accept the challenge—pray for national revival, now!

Additional recommended reading on Charles Finney:
Johnson, Kevin, ed. *Charles G. Finney Lectures on Revival.* Minneapolis: Bethany House Publishers (1988).
Hardman, Keith J. *Charles Grandison Finney 1792-1875, Revivalist and Reformer.* Grand Rapids: Baker Book House Company (1990).
Parkhurst, Louis Gifford Jr., editor and compiler. *Principles of Revival, Charles G. Finney.* Minneapolis: Bethany House Publishers (1987).
(I have included this list after several chapters centered around Charles Finney. I have done this for a few reasons. First, in every case where I have written about Charles Finney, I leaned heavily on these books. Second, the life and ministry of Charles Finney has for generations been the subject of ridicule by many well-meaning religious writers. I would like my readers to check his work out for themselves. Third, if this list is readily available, perhaps my readers will use it as a shopping list the next time they walk through their favorite bookstore.)

Instead of the ill-advised hopes of the last two centuries, which have reduced us to insignificance and brought us to the brink of nuclear and non-nuclear death, we can only reach with determination for the warm hand of God, which we have so rashly and self-confidently pushed away. . . . Man has forgotten God, that is why this has happened.

—Alexandr Solzhenitsyn, Nobel Prize winning Russian author, speaking about the plight of his homeland (AGCEQ).

Chapter 5—Is God judging America?

Historians have repeatedly noted that there have been an unusually high number of calamitous natural disasters over the past two decades. They have included earthquakes, floods, forest fires, hurricanes, El Ninos, La Ninas, etc. The 1990s gave us the worst winter in a hundred years, record Mississippi Valley floods, and the worst forest fires ever recorded. Some have entertained this thought: "Do these and other calamities represent the punishment of God?"

One concerned California pastor declared unequivocally that the California quakes were "not the judgment of God. They were simply the result of the shifting plates of the fragile earth's surface."

He further insisted that because we are not now in what he terms the "dispensation of judgment"; that God will not (or cannot) punish our evil acts on this side of the grave.

I believe that this (or a similar) view is shared by a large segment of Christendom.

I would ask, however, whether this notion is founded on sound biblical evidence, or if it is based more on expedience than hermeneutics?

While it may be just plain frightening to think that God might judge (or chastise) us on this side of the grave, we must not turn our back on what the Bible teaches in this regard. There are several biblical passages that shed light on this subject.

First of all, the New Testament teaches that God is the "same yesterday and today and forever" (Heb. 13:8). That being the case, if God refused to tolerate sin in the days of Sodom and Gomorrah, why should we expect Him to tolerate sin today?

The New Testament also says: "Do not be deceived, God is not mocked; for whatever a man sows, this he will also reap. For the one who sows to his own flesh will from the flesh reap corruption, but the one who sows to the Spirit will from the Spirit reap eternal life" (Gal. 6:7-8).

This "law of the harvest" concept is a popular theme running throughout all of Scripture. What it speaks to is not exclusively end-time judgment, either: "Blessed is the nation whose God is the Lord" (Ps. 33:12). There is no evidence to suggest that there are "nations" in heaven—just here on good old planet earth!

Earlier in this Psalm it states, "The Lord nullifies the counsel of the nations; He frustrates the plans of the peoples. The counsel of the Lord stands forever, The plans of His heart from generation to generation" (Ps. 33:10-11).

In the New Testament, it does sometimes appear that sin goes unpunished in this life. I believe that this is due (at least in part) to the fact that the historical framework of the New Testament comprised such a very short period of time (half a century at the most, as opposed to the one thousand plus years of the Old Testament).

There simply was not a long enough time for the "law of the harvest" fully to be realized in every instance within the limited time frame of the New Testament.

Still, there are instances in the New Testament which do clearly depict the reality and power of God's earthly punishment.

For example, the sin of Legion (the Gerasene Demoniac) rendered him a useless human being: "Constantly, night and day, he was screaming among the tombs and in the mountains, and gashing himself with stones" (Mark 5:5). He was reaping what he had sown.

Certainly, when he first began toying with sin, he was not in such a desperate condition. He probably enjoyed his sin, at first. Certainly, sin has its charms, for a season (even for the demoniac); but its end is always destruction.

In this case, Legion was "punished" this side of the grave. It is clear that the law of the harvest prevailed in the life of Legion.

In the Book of Acts, Ananias stole from God, and then lied to Peter about it. God immediately struck him dead. When his widow parroted the same deceit, God struck her down as well (Acts 5:1ff). As I see it, this represents another instance of punishment, this side of the grave.

Concerning the church at Ephesus, God said: "But I have this against you, that you have left your first love. Therefore remember from where you have fallen, and repent and do the deeds you did at first; or else I am coming to you and will remove your lampstand out of its place—unless you repent" (Rev. 2:4-5).

Deprivation of blessing is nothing less than punishment.

At any rate, it is clear from both the Old and New Testaments that God does punish this side of the grave.

Concerning God's sovereignty over the universe, I believe that it is very dangerous to think that God views the world as a giant wind-up toy that, once He sets it into motion, He simply withholds His hand from its operation. Charles Finney addressed that view of God like this: "There is no natural event in which His own agency is not concerned. He has not built the creation like a vast machine that will go on alone, without His further care. He has not retired from the universe, to let it work for itself. That is mere Deism. He exercises a universal superintendence and control. And yet every event in nature has been brought about by means. He administers neither providence nor grace with that sort of sovereignty that dispenses with the use of means. There is no more sovereignty in the one than in the other" (*Lectures on Revivals of Religion,* Lecture I, 1835).

There are numerous examples of God's sovereignty overruling nature. In the Old Testament, He created all things, established the rainbow as a sign, parted the great waters, burned (but did not consume) the bush, held back the rains in famine, poured them out in times of plenty, and stopped time in its tracks to aid His people during battle.

In the New Testament, God caused the winds to blow, and to cease blowing, He turned the water into wine, rent the veil of the temple with a great earthquake at the very moment Jesus died, and freed Paul and Silas from prison with another great earthquake.

In more recent times, one has only to read American History (from original sources) to see the Hand of God in the affairs of men. Even the British officers acknowledged God's intervention in nature to bring about His goals.

In one instance, the army of General Cornwallis was about to overtake the Continental army at the Dan River in Virginia (Feb. 13, 1781). The Continental Army crossed easily, then a sudden rise in the waters prevented the almost-certain defeat of the Americans. Clinton, the commander-in-chief under Cornwallis, wrote: "Here the royal army was again stopped by a sudden rise of the waters, which had only just fallen (almost miraculously) to let the enemy over, who could not else have eluded Lord Cornwallis' grasp, so close was he upon their rear."

The last great battle between the armies of Washington and Cornwallis again serves as a prime example of God interjecting Himself into the order of nature. In October of 1781, Cornwallis was having a tough time against the combined armies of the Americans and the French. He determined that if he retreated, secretly, across the York River, he could reorganize his forces, and probably escape defeat.

Under the cover of darkness, on the sixteenth of the month, he began his retreat. The first few boats landed safely—it appeared that he was succeeding. But then God entered the picture.

Cornwallis later writes about the events of that evening: "But at this critical moment, the weather, from being moderate and calm, changed to a most violent storm of wind and rain, and drove all the boats, some of which had troops on board, down the river."

When Washington attacked in the morning, the British forces, though still substantial, were divided and easily defeated. This essentially ended the war.

Not only did Cornwallis recognize God's hand in this battle, so did the Americans. The Journals of the Continental Congress record this entry: "Resolved, that Congress will, at two o'clock this day, go in procession to the Dutch Lutheran Church, and return thanks to Almighty God, for crowning the allied arms of the United States and France, with success, by the surrender of the whole British army under the command of the Earl of Cornwallis."

George Washington wrote: "The General congratulates the army upon the glorious event of yesterday. . . . Divine service is to be performed tomorrow in the several brigades and divisions. The commander-in-chief recommends that the troops not on duty should universally attend with that seriousness of deportment and gratitude of heart which the recognition of such reiterated and astonishing interpositions of Providence demand of us."

The American Revolutionary War was born out of revival. It was in every sense a holy war. America had a holy covenant with God from the beginning, and God enforced it.

For the British, those blessings of God, poured out on their enemy, must surely have felt like cursings to them. They must have felt that they were under the terrible judgment hand of God. From their correspondence, it is quite obvious that they were *very* much aware that they were on the wrong side of a holy war.

Concerning God's judgment in the twentieth century, Russian Patriot,

Nobel Prize Winner, and Christian Prophet, Aleksandr Solzhenitsyn, spoke in his Templeton Address: "If I were called upon to identify briefly the principal trait of the entire twentieth century . . . I would be unable to find anything more precise and pithy than to repeat once again: Men have forgotten God. . . . Only a godless embitterment could have moved ostensibly Christian states to employ poison gas, a weapon so obviously beyond the limits of humanity" ("Templeton Address," World Copyright ©1983 by Aleksandr Solzhenitsyn).

Theologian Carl Henry wrote: "Academia must recover the conviction and promulgation of shared values, of which in the West that of God has been supreme above all. Unless it does so, the fading space-time relativities will by default replace what was once the vision of God and of the good, and will doom man to mistake himself and his neighbor for passing shadows in the night, transient oddities with no future but the grave" (Reprinted by permission from *Imprimis*, a publication of Hillsdale College).

Billy Graham wrote years ago: "I see storms of apocalyptic proportion on the horizon. God is trying to get our attention. What next?"

As alluded to earlier, the 1990s was a "decade of plagues." During that time we had our nation's most expensive earthquake ever, our worst hurricane ever, our greatest flooding in six hundred years (Mississippi Valley), our worst drought in six hundred years (California), our worst winter in one hundred years, our worst divorce rate, our worst crime rate, and our lowest academic standards.

Today our children are being taught promiscuity and self-hate against our will; while at the same time our educators turn their backs on crime, drugs, violence, illegitimacy, and low educational standards (Our children are testing the lowest among first world countries!).

Call it the "judgment of God," or simply call it "God withholding His protective covering." The results are the same—lives, homes and families are being destroyed at a fast-forward speed.

Our country's plight stems from this: America is doing business *outside* the providential care of God. In 1962, we, as a political and social entity, formally denied our desire for it. This fact is fully demonstrated through decisions handed down by Earl Warren's Supreme Court at that time.

"Why," I would ask, "should we then be surprised when calamity strikes?"

Were the California quakes the judgment of God? How about our current economic meltdown? Is that the result of the judgment of God? Or what should we think about the never ending wars in which we have become entangled over the past several decades? How about the terror attacks?

Call them whatever you want. The fact remains that God could have prevented them, and He chose not to. It is exactly that simple. America is, without a doubt, under the judgment hand of God.

You can help put an end to this slide.

Accept the challenge—pray for national revival, now!

God who gave us life gave us liberty.
And can the liberties of a nation be thought secure
when we have removed their only firm basis,
a conviction in the minds of the people
that these liberties are the Gift of God?
[That they are not to be violated but with His wrath?]
Indeed, I tremble for my country
when I reflect that God is just;
that His justice cannot sleep forever.

—Thomas Jefferson, Third President of the United States,
and "Author of the Declaration of Independence" (AGCEQ).

Chapter 6—Is God a bad guy?

Does the so-called "judgment of God" make Him a "bad guy?" If God does punish people this side of the grave, and if God does cause (or even *allows*) a certain amount of pain and suffering—does that make Him a bad guy?

Some people think so.

I have heard people say: "Man! Who would want to have anything to do with a god who treats people with such callous disregard? Isn't God supposed to be the God of love? I sure don't think much of that!"

My response to that is simple. It doesn't make a "hill of beans" difference what we think about it. God is God. If He chooses to chastise (or to withhold His protection), He may, in His sovereignty, do just that! And He can do it with or without our permission.

In fact, God says that when He does correct us, He does it for our own good, because He loves us: "Those whom I love, I reprove and discipline" (Rev. 3:19).

Furthermore, it is clear from history that holiness is far more readily attained under duress than comfort. The Church grew during times of oppression, and languished in days of ease. It has always been that way. Look at how the Church advanced during Paul's lifetime. He was imprisoned many times, at least once in a sewer! It is obvious that God was not overly concerned about Paul's physical comfort. Why should He be concerned about our relative comfort?

Concerning hard times, Paul wrote: "For I have learned to be content in whatever circumstances I am . . . in any and every circumstance I have learned the secret of being filled and going hungry" (Phil. 4:11-12). He referred to these problems as "momentary, light affliction" (2 Cor. 4:17).

Why would we think that God should regard our personal comfort more highly than that of Joseph, Paul, Peter, Stephen, or John the Baptist? For that matter, God was not even too considerate about the sensitivities or reputation of His own Son! There was a dirty job to do, and the Son of God was assigned to do it.

The questions to be asked are not: "Are we comfortable enough? Do we have enough to eat? Do we have enough money? Are we safe from foreign invasion?"

No, the questions we should ask ourselves are these: "Have we totally submitted ourselves to the will of God today? Have we accomplished the work He assigned us for today? Are we holding anything back from God? Do we relish any sin?"

These are the real questions.

Our reward, after all, is not in this life. The Bible does not teach us to be concerned at all about our own welfare on earth.

"Who were they," I would ask, "'that did not love their life even when faced with death'" (Rev. 12:11)?

Today, as I sit here writing these words, I have just read about a Christian leader who is imprisoned in Iran. He has been in jail, under a sentence of imminent death, for many years. His crime was preaching the gospel.

At one of his more recent trials the judge required him to testify in his own defense. He came forward and delivered a most eloquent presentation.

His words, however, did not offer any impassioned plea for mercy for himself. He made no apologies. He did not request a larger cell.

No, his plea was only for the salvation of his captors; and his praises were only to God. He was thankful for God's love and His grace.

Are we, in America, afraid of discomfort or death? Do we now believe that death might actually have a sting? Do we think that the grave can now defeat us?

Let's face it—pain and death are universal. They eventually get us all. Jesus said, "do not worry about your life" (Luke 12:22).

Anyway, how many people do we personally know who got out of this thing with their earthly bodies intact? Or, even their fortunes? Did you ever see a hearse pulling a trailer?

The fact is that discomfort, pain, death, or the loss of personal property, must not be regarded as problems for us—not if we truly have our treasures on the other side. Our only concern this side of the grave must be sin—personal and corporate.

God does love us, and He does chastise us. The law of the harvest (the seeds you plant turn into the crops you grow) prevails. God will judge America.

The only recourse for America is total repentance (2 Chronicles 7:14). God is a God of mercy. He spared Nineveh when they repented. He will spare America if we repent.

If, however, we maintain our present course, I am convinced He will allow our destruction.

In fact, I believe that for God to continue to overlook the evil in our land today, He would have to retrieve Sodom and Gomorrah from the depths of the Dead Sea, restore the Roman Empire, and then recall His Book for revision.

God is a loving God—it is for this very reason that He will not let this nation continue on its present course.

There is no doubt that the God of judgment is good.

Accept the challenge—pray for national revival, now!

*I have examined all religions,
as well as my narrow sphere, my straightened means,
and my busy life, would allow;
and the result is that the Bible is the
best Book in the world.
It contains more philosophy
than all the libraries I have seen. . . .
The Ten Commandments
and the Sermon on the Mount
contain my religion. . . .
As I understand the Christian religion,
it was, and is, a revelation.*

—John Adams, Second President of the United States,
and the first to live in the White House (AGCEQ).

Chapter 7—Conversation with a Baptist preacher

I said, "The Body of Christ needs unity. We have got to get together, or we will *never* see revival."

Jim replied, "That may be true, but only to a degree."

I did not respond to his comment. At first I was angry. How could anyone suggest that the body of Christ needs only a "degree" of unity!

I pondered his comment for hours. After a time, my anger turned to pity. "That poor, confused guy," I thought. That line of thinking, however, quickly failed me. I knew that Jim was neither pitiful nor confused. His credentials were impeccable. For nearly twenty years Jim served the Lord as a pastor. Then for the next decade and a half he worked as a home missionary.

In this second stage of his ministry he had invested his time and energies helping new ministries get started. With his own two hands Jim had help build numerous churches all across the country. I had a real problem—Jim was sincere, his ministry legitimate, and his character above reproach. Yet, I could not agree with him on this single matter.

I spent many long hours in prayer and thought, trying to grapple with Jim's comment. Finally, it dawned on me just what he was he was getting at. While his choice of words could have been chosen better, his line of thinking was *entirely* correct.

Truly, our efforts ought not be to unify denominations. That's the mistake made by the ecumenical movement. It sought, strictly on the human level, to find common ground for the entire Christian Church— if a person wore a cross around his neck, his views must somehow be accommodated. That effort was destined for failure from the beginning.

The only way we will ever accomplish total unity in the body of Christ is to draw closer to Jesus. The dynamic here is this: as we draw near to Jesus, we will draw nearer to each other. All efforts on the human level are doomed.

Consider this imagery: Imagine a large, capital "A." Picture your denomination at the base of one of the legs of that capital "A," and one of the other denominations at the base of the other leg. At the top of the "A" is God. All efforts to draw the two legs in towards the middle are going to fail. If they are drawn in, the figure will cease to be stable, it will topple, and it will no longer approach God.

If, however, the denominations first seek after God, they will just naturally migrate up the structure towards Him, the structure will maintain its integrity, and they will quite naturally come together in Him—for He is One. But *only* if they do not grow tired and seek shortcuts.

Obviously, my word picture oversimplifies the process, but I think it helps explain it just the same.

The differences will remain, but those differences just won't matter anymore. I think the songwriter best described it with these words: "Look full in His wonderful face, And the things of earth will grow strangely dim, In the light of His glory and grace" (Helen H. Lemmel, 1922).

Revival will draw us together in unity. However, that "togetherness" must not be the torch we follow. True unity (revival unity) will occur only as we draw closer to Him.

Jim, I now see what you mean. Thanks for pointing it out to me.

Accept the challenge—pray for national revival, now!

Chapter 8—Where do you suppose revival will start in America?

One of most popular topics of conversation (among baby boomers) is, "Where were you when Kennedy was shot?"

If there is one thing that strikes a cord in those born in the 1940s and 1950s, it is that event. Almost everyone of that generation can tell you where he was, and what he was doing, when Kennedy was passing in front of Dealey Plaza on that fateful Dallas day.

My prayer is that a similar reaction will be common to this generation. Not, however, in reaction to "where were you when someone was shot?" But "where were you when the 'Big One' hit?"

By "Big One," I am referring to the Big Revival (the Third Great Awakening).

While there is certainly a great deal of intercession going on in America right now, along with a lot of anticipation, I think that it is fair to say that the big wave of the "Third Great Awakening" has not yet made it to land.

My question is: When it does arrive, where do you suppose it will hit?

While I do not know where or when revival will come to America, I do know one thing for certain about it: When the great revival does arrive, it will do so through human agency. That's just the way God works—He always uses human flesh.

It is also certain that the Spirit of God will avoid pretentious religion. He will come to a humble people. In every recorded case of revival, the Church was first prepared, through repentance and humility, for the outpouring of the Spirit of God.

So, regarding the "where" and "when"—I don't have a clue. But I do know about the "how."

Martin Luther began his preaching in a tumbledown building in Wittenberg. The building stood in the middle of the town square. It was a very old wooden chapel, measuring thirty feet by twenty feet. Its walls were on the verge of collapsing, having to be propped up on all sides.

John and Charles Wesley would walk from one poor church to the next, sometimes preaching in nine poor churches in a single week!

Charles Finney first preached in schools, taverns, halls and factories, as well as in small out-of-the-way churches.

Jeremiah Lamphier preached on street corners in New York. Only six people attended his first prayer meeting. Within six months, tens of thousands were praying with him!

The great Welsh Revival started under the ministry of poor preachers who went out into the rugged workplaces of the hard-working coal miners.

So, I will repeat my question: When it does arrive, where do you suppose it will hit first? Where is the next big wave of revival going to strike? Perhaps in the prisons. Could that be? Perhaps in the hospital wards. I've heard that suggested. Perhaps in a simple college dorm room. How about among the drug culture? Perhaps revival will break out in the drug rehab programs.

Of course, revival doesn't have to follow any historic pattern. But, I think that it is highly likely that revival will again bury its roots in simple surroundings.

I am convinced that it will establish its home among humble, hungry people. It will come to those who are diligently seeking it through repentance and intercession.

Maybe, just maybe, the big revival will strike first in those prayer meetings that you and your friends have started. The ones you intended to be a half-hour long, but instead, they turned out to last hours, or perhaps even all night long. Maybe they will provide the opening that the Holy Spirit seeks!

Perhaps it will be upon the soil made rich by your tears that the Spirit of God will pour out His blessings of revival this time!

Keep praying—revival is coming.

If you have not already accepted the challenge, do it now!

God hasn't called me to be successful.
He's called me to be faithful.
We can do no great things,
only small things with great love.
If you want to pray better,
you must pray more.

—Mother Teresa of Calcutta (AGCEQ).

Chapter 9—Praying moms

One of the greatest revivals in history occurred under the ministry of two brothers, John and Charles Wesley. Not since Martin Luther had the world been so shaken by the power of God.

As is the case with nearly all immensely productive men, the Wesley brothers were most strongly influenced in life by their mother. The mother of John and Charles was a powerful woman of prayer. As the wife of a poor minister of the gospel, and mother of nineteen children, she experienced great difficulty finding either time or a place for prayer.

But she persisted. She made it a daily practice to pray for each one of her children, individually. Because she had no empty space in her tiny house, when she wanted to pray, she simply threw her apron over her head, in the middle of her family, in the middle of the day. Mom Wesley created her own prayer closet.

It was through those mighty, life-changing prayers, that John and Charles received strength for their nation-changing revival. I wonder how many praying moms we have in our country today. I think we might be surprised to learn just how many moms are now praying, daily and diligently, for their children.

I know personally the power of a mother's prayer. When I was a teenager I can remember every night hearing my mother praying for me in the living room; often many hours into the night. When I would get up to use the restroom I would see her on her knees at the couch. It had a strong effect on me.

Moms—please do not wait around for someone else to start revival in your home. Do not believe that you can flip through the TV channels until you latch on to someone else's "revival." *Real* revival will never start in the TV room—it starts in the prayer closet. And, remember, a prayer closet can be any place where you can shut yourself up with God.

That's all it takes. If you call it a prayer closet, it's a prayer closet. It doesn't matter if it's no more than an apron over your head, it counts.

I believe that we will have nation-changing revival in our beloved America when more of God's moms have pulled aprons over their heads.

Accept the challenge—pray for national revival, now!

Chapter 10—Mostly Maria prayed

(This account was paraphrased largely from a book edited by Garth M. Rosell and Richard A.G. Dupuis, *The Memoirs of Charles G. Finney*. Grand Rapids: Zondervan Publishing House (1989) pp. 232-240 Additional suggested reading on Charles Finney at end of this chapter.)

Maria rose up from her seat and approached the exhausted Charles Finney just as he was walking out from behind the pulpit.

With tears in her eyes, she asked the preacher: "Rev. Finney, would you please come and preach in my city? I live in Stephentown. And it is only a few miles down the road. Would you come and preach there?"

Finney looked at the young girl and smiled. While he sympathized with her concern, Finney explained that he would have to decline the request because his hands were already too full with the revival in New Lebanon.

The next Sunday Maria petitioned Finney again. And again Finney explained that while he would like to come to Stephentown, he still must refuse her offer.

"But, Mr. Finney, if you knew anything of the state of things in Stephentown, you would surely come," Maria persisted.

Finney paused for a moment to probe the girl's spirit. Looking deeply into the girl's tear-stained eyes, he replied, "Next week. If you will locate an appropriate place to meet, I will come to Stephentown and preach then, but only after I have preached my two Sabbath sermons in New Lebanon. I finish up here about 5 p.m."

Maria was ecstatic. She bounded out of the church and headed home to prepare the way for Finney.

The next Sunday Maria greeted Finney as he arrived in Stephentown, and accompanied him to her father's house. Mr. Sackett (Maria's father) showed Finney to a private room where he could pray alone before preaching. As Finney began to pray, he could hear the plaintive intercession offered up in the room directly above his. It was Maria. Sobbing and weeping, the girl cried out in the greatest of agony for the lost people in her town.

After the service (which was unproductive in Finney's eyes), the revivalist returned to the Sackett house to spend the night. Again Finney was moved by the sounds of Maria's praying in the room above. The young girl prayed all night long.

It was to the credit of Maria's spirit of prayer that Finney agreed to return the next week, and then a third week.

It was not until the end of the service on this third Sunday night that God moved on the people of Stephentown. As Finney left the pulpit, Maria called him over to talk to a young lady who was under conviction. Her name was Henrietta Platt, the daughter of a very prominent judge.

Henrietta immediately gave her heart to God. From that day on those two young ladies, Henrietta and Maria, bonded themselves together in a union of prayer that changed their whole community forever, and, to a degree, changed the whole nation.

It was at that time, after the third week, Finney was captivated by the spirit of prayer that seemed to rule Maria's life. So much so that he closed out his meetings in New Lebanon, and moved his entire ministry to Stephentown! Maria and Henrietta prayed without ceasing, and Finney preached under the powerful anointing of the Holy Spirit.

In his description of the events in Stephentown, Finney recounts that the most powerful men in the area were "rendered entirely helpless" by the power of God. Many had to be carried home after the Holy Spirit had fallen upon them.

One prominent lawyer of the time, Mr. Zebulon Shipherd, upon hearing about the unusual events surrounding the revival preaching of Finney, traveled a long distance to visit one of Finney's services. He was so taken up with the revival, he disposed of his lucrative practice, and joined Finney in the work.

The revival grew stronger and stronger, so that before Finney left Stephentown nearly every single person in the entire area had accepted God.

Many of the people saved under Finney in Stephentown later became effective ministers of the gospel. Henrietta Platt met and married Almon Underwood. Together they ignited revival fires throughout New Jersey and New England.

J. J. Shipherd, the son of Zebulon Shipherd, went on to found two world-renown centers of Christian education in the Midwest: Oberlin College in Ohio, and Olivet College in Michigan. These two colleges alone produced thousands of pastors, evangelists, missionaries and Christian lay leaders.

But what about Maria? Did she ever become famous?

The answer is, "No." You will not read much about Maria in history books. You will not find her name chiseled in a granite cornerstone. Such is not the fate of an intercessor. And that is exactly what Maria was—an intercessor.

Fortunately, Charles Finney recognized that fact when he looked deeply into Maria's eyes. He could see that she had been with God. He knew she was an intercessor. And he, more than any of his contemporaries, knew the value of intercessory prayer. He knew that there could be no revival without it!

God, please send us more girls like Maria! Please send us intercessors! Please send us revival!

Accept the challenge—pray for national revival, now!

Recommended reading on Charles Finney:

Johnson, Kevin, ed. *Charles G. Finney Lectures on Revival.* Minneapolis: Bethany House Publishers (1988).

Richard A.G. Dupuis, *The Memoirs of Charles G. Finney.* Grand Rapids: Zondervan Publishing House (1989)

Hardman, Keith J. *Charles Grandison Finney 1792-1875, Revivalist and Reformer.* Grand Rapids: Baker Book House Company (1990).

Parkhurst, Louis Gifford Jr., editor and compiler. *Principles of Revival, Charles G. Finney.* Minneapolis: Bethany House Publishers (1987).

(I have included this list after several chapters centered around Charles Finney. I have done this for a few reasons. First, in every case where I have written about Charles Finney, I leaned heavily on these books. Second, the life and ministry of Charles Finney has for generations been the subject of ridicule by many well-meaning religious writers. I would like my readers to check his work out for themselves. Third, if this list is readily available, perhaps my readers will use it as a shopping list the next time they walk through their favorite bookstore.)

Chapter 11—Max Memry's diary (a "conversation" with Ben Franklin)

Dear Diary: I had lunch today with one of the most interesting people I have ever met—Mr. Benjamin Franklin. I could have asked him a thousand questions. However, I limited my interview this day to his notion of religion, as it related to education.

Max: Mr. Franklin, everyone knows about your manifold talents. In fact, you may be the most respected man in the world. Would you tell me, please, should a young man be taught religion?

Franklin: I think that nothing is of more importance for the public weal, than to form and train up youth in wisdom and virtue. I think, moreover, that talents for the education of youth are the gift of God; and that he on whom they are bestowed, whenever a way is opened for the use of them, is as strongly called as if he heard a voice from heaven.

Max: Let me get this straight. Are you saying that young people need to be taught virtue *even above* the standard academic disciplines?

Franklin: Only a virtuous people are capable of freedom.

Max: That being the case, what do you consider to be the pillars of that virtue?

Franklin: A Bible and a newspaper in every house, a good school in every district—all studied and appreciated as they merit—are the principal support of virtue, morality, and civil liberty.

Max: Mr. Franklin, do you consider yourself a religious man?

Franklin: I never doubted the existence of the Deity; that he made the world, and governed it by his Providence; that the most acceptable service of God was the doing good to man; that our souls are immortal, and that all crime will be punished, and virtue rewarded, either here or hereafter.

Max: Do you believe that reliance on God is vital to this new nation; especially in consideration of the potential enemies residing without, and the dangers within?

Franklin: It is the duty of mankind on all suitable occasions to acknowledge their dependence on the Divine Being, [that] Almighty God would mercifully interpose and still the rage of war among the nations, [and that] He would take this province under His protection, confound the designs and defeat the attempts of its enemies, and unite our hearts and strengthen our hands in every undertaking that may be for the public good, and for our defense and security in this time of danger.

Max: Along this same line, Mr. Franklin, what advice would you give to the future generations of America's leaders?

Franklin: I have lived, Sir, a long time, and the longer I live, the more convincing proofs I see of this truth—that God governs in the affairs of men. And if a sparrow cannot fall to the ground without His notice, is it probable that an empire can rise without His aid?

We have been assured, Sir, in the Sacred Writings, that "except the Lord build the house, they labor in vain that build it." I firmly believe this; and I also believe that without his concurring aid we shall succeed in this political building no better than the builders of Babel: We shall be divided by our partial local interests; our projects will be confounded, and we ourselves shall become a reproach and a byword down to future ages.

Max: It is well known that you are a very close friend of revivalist George Whitefield. I would like to ask you, is that friendship strictly on the human level, or do you support Rev. Whitefield's revival message to the American people?

Franklin: It was wonderful to see the change soon made in the manners of our inhabitants. From being thoughtless or indifferent about religion, it seemed as if all the world were growing religious, so that one could not walk through the town in an evening without hearing psalms sung in different families of every street.

I sometimes wish that he and I had been jointly employed by the Crown to settle a colony on the Ohio, to settle in that fine country a strong body of religious and industrious people! Might it not greatly have facilitated the introduction of pure religion among the heathen, if we could, by such a colony, show them a better sample of Christians than they commonly saw in our Indian traders?

Max: Does this mean you think that revived Christianity can have a major effect on the whole nation?

Franklin: Whoever shall introduce into public affairs the principles of primitive Christianity will change the face of the world.

Max: Mr. Franklin, thank you very much for your consideration, and for your very helpful words. I have greatly enjoyed chatting with you. I look forward to the next time.

(All the words attributed to Mr. Benjamin Franklin in this "virtual interview" are quoted verbatim from his numerous writings.)

Join George Whitefield and Benjamin Franklin:

Accept the challenge—pray for national revival, now!

I think, moreover, that talents
for the education of youth
are the gift of God;
and that he on whom they are bestowed,
whenever a way is opened for the use of them,
is as strongly called
as if he heard a voice from heaven.

—Benjamin Franklin, Senior Statesman,
Diplomat, Inventor, Publisher and Scientist (AGCEQ).

Chapter 12—Ben Franklin had an answer

In 1774, Benjamin Franklin wrote to friends in Europe describing his beloved America: "Bad examples to youth are more rare in America; which must be a comfortable consideration to parents. . . . Atheism is unknown there, infidelity rare and secret; so that persons may live to a great age in that country without having their piety shocked by meeting with either an atheist or an infidel."

Things have changed in America—dramatically. Atheism reigns supreme in our public schools today, and "infidels" pass out condoms to our children. If a child in America survives the womb, when he enters school he is faced with the weapons of drugs and despair. No wonder suicide is a leading cause of death among our young people. Forget about having their "piety shocked," today our children are lucky just to "live to a great age."

America needs national revival. We need to get back to the basics of our religious American roots. We need to revisit Franklin's America— where "bad examples to youth are more rare."

How do we do it? We won't do it by passing new laws; neither will it be accomplished by electing a "righteous" president.

We must do Revelation 2:4. We must go back to our "first love."

Accept the challenge—pray for national revival, now!

In 1904,
Congress declared
"that there be printed and bound,
. . . for the use of Congress,
9,000 copies of Thomas Jefferson's
Morals of Jesus of Nazareth,
as the same appears in the National Museum;
3,000 copies for the use of the Senate
and 6,000 copies for the use of the House."

—Thomas Jefferson, Third President of the United States,
and author of the Declaration of Independence (AGCEQ).

Chapter 13—Thomas Jefferson was actually a card-carrying Christian

Most historical revisionists (and, for the most part, the educational system as a whole) point to Thomas Jefferson and Thomas Paine to establish their argument that our nation was established by non-Christians, thus on non-Christian principles.

While it is true that a good argument can be made for the anti-Christian bias of Thomas Paine, such cannot be said for Thomas Jefferson. Here are some of the things we know about Thomas Jefferson:

As a leader of Virginia, Jefferson introduced a resolution for a Day of Fasting and Prayer; as President of the University of Virginia, he set up a Christian Education program, and built a chapel in which to worship Christ; as School Board President of DC, he authored a curriculum using the Bible and Watt's Christian Hymnal as the *only* reading texts; he signed into law an act "for Propagating the Gospel Among the heathen;" he proposed treaties that built churches and hired and supported Christian preachers for the Indians; he called the Bible the "cornerstone of liberty;" and he translated the Bible into easy, condensed English, to serve as a simple textbook for the education and conversion of American Indians.

Of his own beliefs, Jefferson wrote with his own hand: "My views are very different from that anti-Christian system imputed to me by those who know nothing of my opinions. To the corruptions of Christianity I am indeed opposed, but not to the genuine precepts of Jesus himself. I am a Christian."

Patrick Henry knew Jefferson and the other founders personally. He wrote: "It cannot be emphasized too strongly or too often that this great nation was founded, not by religionists, but by Christians, not on religions but on the gospel of Jesus Christ."

Jefferson claimed to be a Christian, he did a lot of "Christian things," and Patrick Henry supported his contention that he was, indeed, a Christian. I, for one, believe them both!

That leaves Thomas Paine. Regarding that, you must remember, even Jesus had His Judas!

Accept the challenge—pray for national revival, now!

Chapter 14—*Just how close can we get to God?*

Is there a limit, do you suppose, as to just how far we can go in God? Could there be some natural barrier that somehow automatically pops up whenever we start to get too close to Him?

That's the way it is with royalty, you know. Remember when Queen Elizabeth was greeted by Australian Prime Minister Paul Keating in 1992? He committed the ultimate gaffe by hugging the queen. The incident came to be known as the "Lizard of Oz" scandal. The Prime Minister simply got *too* close!

I have heard that British royalty sends out "advance men" to teach the public the proper way to act around the royal family. This envoy instructs those about to meet royalty along this line: "Do not touch members of the royal family, try not to make lingering eye contact (but if you do, smile but don't stare). Do not drink water from a plastic bottle in their presence, quit eating when they do, and do not ask them questions."

Do you suppose that God might employ a similar protocol? Do you think that perhaps God stations angels around His throne to prevent people from pressing in too closely? What does the Bible teach about this?

This is what the Bible says: "Draw near to God and He will draw near to you" (James 4:8). In the Old Testament, God says many times that His people ought to seek His face (2 Chronicles). Later He says, "You will seek Me and find Me when you search for Me with all your heart. I will be found by you, . . . and I will restore your fortunes" (Jer. 29:13-14).

What does that mean? How do we look for Him with "all" our heart?

This just means we must have clean hands and a pure heart, and that we must then pursue His face with everything that is in us (James 4:8ff).

Do we have to be "perfect" to find God?

No. What it means is that we must sincerely repent of every sin, and relish no sin in our hearts. Simply stated—we must surrender our will to His.

What's the payback on this? If we do submit ourselves to God, and seek His face, what's in it for us?

The answer is simple: relationship. As we surrender to God, humble ourselves, repent, and seek His face; He will reveal Himself to us, and He will reveal to us just who we are with relation to Him.

It is awesome!

It is also amazing! It is the most refreshing experience we can imagine. All of the junk that has attached itself to us since last we approached His throne is washed away as we draw near to Him. All worries, fears, dreads, hates, hurts and insecurities are evaporated by His smile.

God's protocol is simple and direct: "Seek, and you will find; knock, and it will be opened to you. For everyone who asks receives, and he who seeks finds, and to him who knocks it will be opened" (Matt. 7:7f).

Just how close can we get to God?

We alone determine that. We are His kids—He will not turn us away.

I guarantee that the only stop signs we will ever encounter on the road to God will be found in our own feeble, insecure, little minds.

Accept the challenge—pray for national revival, now!

Chapter 15—A tale of two revivals

At the beginning of the twentieth century, two revivals were occurring simultaneously—one on the west coast of the United States, and the other across the Atlantic in Wales. I found the similarities between the two revivals to be fascinating:

For starters, only those who were willing to completely surrender to the Spirit of God were able to be involved in either of the revivals. They waited on God, and prayed unceasingly.

Prayer meetings continued daily, for weeks on end, day and night. Though the surroundings were humble, they were never closed or empty. They believed in God's promises.

They both described their experiences as "soul travail," much like labor pains at childbirth.

Certain individuals emerged from each of the revivals with the "call to revival." These few prayed day and night, with extended periods of fasting and prayer.

Sectarian prejudices diminished. Unity in the Spirit was sought, but not with ecumenical compromise.

Deep repentance was an important part of both revivals. This phenomenon was evidenced by great volumes of tears, groanings and intercession.

The meetings were led by the Spirit of God. The pastor could enter the meeting, or leave—the meeting would continue in the same manner whether or not he was there. Human leadership was nominal. God ran the proceedings.

Sermons were *not* prepared in advance. Testimony, prayer and praise were intermingled throughout the service. Humility reigned supreme.

Sermons were often "preached" from the rear of the church, or from under a pew.

William Seymour (California) most often preached while on his knees, with his head in a wooden egg crate. Evan Roberts (Wales) wept more than he preached. When he did rise to speak, it would be from off the floor, often from the back of the church.

Excesses were expected and tolerated. This created a great deal of bad press. However, this bad press was not feared in the least. Since the revivalists could not afford "real" advertising, the notoriety served that purpose.

"For two hours at midday all Denver was held in a spell. . . . The marts of trade were deserted . . . and all worldly affairs were forgotten, and the entire city was given over to meditation of higher things . . . an entire great city, in the middle of a busy weekday, bowing before the throne of heaven" (*Denver Post*, January 20, 1905).

It is a simple fact that when God is on the move, nothing can stop Him—certainly not a little negative media coverage! Tracts and pamphlets were commonly used, but musical instruments and hymn books were discarded, since they were viewed as distractions.

For the most part, all talk was to God, not to the flesh. The thought was that when God was present, who could ignore Him? Personalities were downplayed.

Missionary zeal flourished. All believers were called to a one hundred percent consecration.

In both revivals, revival fire did not fall until their hearts were prepared for it. Otherwise, they believed, it would have been "born prematurely," and would have died.

Accept the challenge—pray for national revival, now!

Chapter 16—1905 prayer meeting

The setting of the 1905 prayer meeting was the First Baptist Church, in Los Angeles, California. The following article (detailing the event) appeared in the *Pasadena Daily News* in 1905. It was entitled, "What I Saw in a Los Angeles Church." The article was written by Frank Bartleman.

For some weeks special services have been held in the First Baptist Church, Los Angeles. Pastor Smale has returned from Wales, where he was in touch with Evan Roberts, and the revival. He registers his conviction that Los Angeles will soon be shaken by the mighty power of God!

The service of which I am writing began impromptu and spontaneous, some time before the pastor arrived. A handful of people had gathered early, which seemed to be sufficient for the Spirit's operation. The meeting started. Their expectation was from God. God was there, the people were there, and by the time the pastor arrived the meeting was in full swing. Pastor Smale dropped into his place, but no one seemed to pay any especial attention to him. Their minds were on God. No one seemed to get in another's way, although the congregation represented many religious bodies. All seemed perfect harmony.

The pastor arose, read a portion of the Scripture, made a few well chosen remarks full of hope and inspiration for the occasion, and the meeting passed again from his hands. The people took it up and went on as before. Testimony, prayer and praise were intermingled throughout the service. The meeting seemed to run itself as far as human guidance was concerned. The pastor was one of them. If one is at all impressionable religiously he must feel in such an atmosphere that something wonderful and imminent is about to take place. Some mysterious, mighty upheaval in the spiritual world is evidently at our doors. The meeting gives one a feeling of 'heaven on earth,' with an assurance that the supernatural exists, and that in a very real sense.

Well, revival did come to First Baptist Church. For months they held prayer meetings and evangelistic services, seven days a week!

Accept the challenge—pray for national revival, now!

The best work that I found on this revival is Bartleman, Frank. *Azusa Street*. Plainfield, New Jersey: Logos International (1925). The above account is recorded in Bartleman's book

Chapter 17—Met any loud bartenders lately?

Charles Finney was fond of telling the story of a special intercessor from the northern part of New York State.

This gentleman kept a list of unsaved people for whom he constantly prayed. The names on his list were considered the toughest to win over— the hardened, abandoned and unreachable.

Once, upon arriving at a small country town in which revival was just beginning, he ran face-to-face into a particularly difficult unbeliever—the local tavern owner.

Whenever this scoffer would encounter a Christian, or even see one walking across the street, he would burst forth in his most boisterous voice, spouting out line upon line of expletives and God cursing.

He made sure every Christian in town was greeted in this manner. Soon all the churchgoers found new ways to get across town, avoiding at all cost walking within sight of this obnoxious character.

Finney's intercessor put this tavern owner at the top of his prayer list, and agonized for him in prayer day and night.

It wasn't very long, tells Finney, that this rebellious fellow came to a meeting, got up, confessed his sins and came to God.

The bartender then closed his tavern to all except the intercessory prayer warriors!

It was then that the really deep revival waters flowed through that town!

Finney describes this type of prayer in these words: "The Spirit leads Christians to want and pray for things not specifically mentioned in the Bible. . . . Here the Spirit comes to lead Christians to pray for certain individuals at certain times when God is prepared to bless them. When we don't know what to pray for, the Holy Spirit leads our minds to think about some object, contemplate its situation and value, and to feel for it and pray and labor in birth until the person is converted."

How about you? Ask God to lay some stubborn sinner on your heart. Then pray him through to salvation. Don't give up until he surrenders his heart to God.

Perhaps it will be the local bartender. Or, maybe it will be a close relative!

Accept the challenge—pray for national revival, now!

Recommended reading on Charles Finney:
Johnson, Kevin, ed. *Charles G. Finney Lectures on Revival.* Minneapolis: Bethany House Publishers (1988).
Richard A.G. Dupuis, *The Memoirs of Charles G. Finney.* Grand Rapids: Zondervan Publishing House (1989)
Hardman, Keith J. *Charles Grandison Finney 1792-1875, Revivalist and Reformer.* Grand Rapids: Baker Book House Company (1990).
Parkhurst, Louis Gifford Jr., editor and compiler. *Principles of Revival, Charles G. Finney.* Minneapolis: Bethany House Publishers (1987).
(I have included this list after several chapters centered around Charles Finney. I have done this for a few reasons. First, in every case where I have written about Charles Finney, I leaned heavily on these books. Second, the life and ministry of Charles Finney has for generations been the subject of ridicule by many well-meaning religious writers. I would like my readers to check his work out for themselves. Third, if this list is readily available, perhaps my readers will use it as a shopping list the next time they walk through their favorite bookstore.)

Chapter 18—Formula for revival

During the early days of the great Welsh Revival (1904) a Wilshire evangelist visited a meeting at Ferndale, at which the Revival's leader, Evan Roberts, was presiding.

The visitor stood up and asked, "Friends, I have journeyed into Wales with the hope that I may glean the secret of the Welsh Revival?"

Evan Roberts reputedly stood to his feet, lifted his arm toward the visitor, and replied that there was no secret! It was a matter of asking and receiving.

Charles Finney (1840) said: "Just as far as our own country (America) falls further into unbelief neither God nor human beings can further Christianity except through powerful awakenings. God has always worked in this way."

He continued: "Revival is not dependent on a miracle in any sense. It is a result we can logically expect from the right use of God-given means, as much as any other effect produced by applying tools and resources."

Concerning the coldness of the Church in his day Finney said: "Christians are more to blame for not being revived than sinners are for not being converted."

There is an inhibiting spirit prevalent in American churches today which leads us to expect revival only once in a lifetime, or perhaps even less frequent. Finney thought that idea was absurd. He believed we should have revival whenever we were "unrevived"—he suggested revival every three or four days, if we can wait that long!

He fought the notion that revival was somehow "mysteriously a subject of God's sovereignty." He held that we must "remember one fact about God's government: the most necessary things are the most easily obtained when we use the appointed means." He compared seeking revival to a farmer planting a seed—both belonged to the category of "cause and effect."

How do we plant revival seeds? We do 2 Chronicles 7:14.

If we truly want revival, we must follow the example of the successful revivalists of the past.

Let's start planting revival seeds today!

Accept the challenge—pray for national revival, now!

Recommended reading on Charles Finney:

Johnson, Kevin, ed. *Charles G. Finney Lectures on Revival.* Minneapolis: Bethany House Publishers (1988).

Richard A.G. Dupuis, *The Memoirs of Charles G. Finney.* Grand Rapids: Zondervan Publishing House (1989)

Hardman, Keith J. *Charles Grandison Finney 1792-1875, Revivalist and Reformer.* Grand Rapids: Baker Book House Company (1990).

Parkhurst, Louis Gifford Jr., editor and compiler. *Principles of Revival, Charles G. Finney.* Minneapolis: Bethany House Publishers (1987).

(I have included this list after several chapters centered around Charles Finney. I have done this for a few reasons. First, in every case where I have written about Charles Finney, I leaned heavily on these books. Second, the life and ministry of Charles Finney has for generations been the subject of ridicule by many well-meaning religious writers. I would like my readers to check his work out for themselves. Third, if this list is readily available, perhaps my readers will use it as a shopping list the next time they walk through their favorite bookstore.)

Chapter 19—Lightning-rod revival

Lightning-rod revival refers to the concept of revival that views man as the passive recipient of the "blessing" of revival, as opposed to the active seeker of God's presence.

That is to say, man is like a lightning rod waiting for God to "pop" him, perhaps suddenly and unexpectedly, with a bolt of His revival "lightning."

Those who hold to this notion believe that revival is so sovereign a work of God, that Christians ought not even intercede for it. "Christians cannot," they would say, "pray down revival."

The ultimate conclusion of this argument is that "it's God's fault, not man's, that the Church is unrevived. When God wants to send revival to the Church, He will! Until then, it is man's job to stand by and passively wait for the so-called 'promise' of revival."

The relevant question here is this: "What does the Bible teach about man's role in revival?"

The Bible says, "If . . . My people who are called by My name humble themselves and pray and seek My face and turn from their wicked ways, then I will hear from heaven, and will forgive their sin and will heal their land" (2 Chron. 7:13-14).

The Prophet Joel writes: "Consecrate a fast, Proclaim a solemn assembly; Gather the elders And all the inhabitants of the land To the house of the Lord your God, And cry out to the Lord. Alas for the day! For the day of the Lord is near" (Joel 1:14-15). Later Joel writes: "'Yet even now,' declares the Lord, 'Return to Me with all your heart, And with fasting, weeping and mourning; And rend your heart and not your garments.' Now return to the Lord your God" (2:12-13).

Clearly, the Bible teaches the *active* notion of revival.

What, then, does *history* teach about revival? Can a case there be made for a passive lightning-rod type revival? The powerful revival leaders (those such as D.L. Moody, William Booth, Evan Roberts, Charles Finney, John and Charles Wesley, etc.) all strongly advocated revival praying. In fact, everyone who was ever used by God (in revival) believed that revival comes about only through prayer and repentance. I find no exception to that rule—they all taught that man's role in revival was an active one! None of them suggested so much as a hint in favor of human passivity with regard to revival.

Because it is clear that both the Bible and history teach an active role for the Church in facilitating revival; why, then, do some professors of religion still teach that man's role in revival is passive, like that of a lightning rod?

I can think of only two possible reasons for such a view. The first reason being that they have failed to study properly. For whatever reason, they have not diligently studied the Word of God concerning revival; neither have they objectively approached history from an original source standpoint.

The second possibility for such a skewed view is even less virtuous: Perhaps they simply do not want to pay the price of revival. I suggest that it is possible that their pride will not allow them to humble themselves, and pray, and seek God's face, and turn from their own wicked ways.

Rather than repent, perhaps they simply choose to stand back and self-assuredly blame God for the terrible condition of the Church in this land.

Whatever be the case, the time has come for the Church to take a reality pill; it is time to wake up. The condition of the Church today is the direct result of this passive notion of Christianity.

It's a simple fact—there is no such thing as "lightning-rod revival!"

Only those who actively seek revival can facilitate it. Revival praying, and *only* revival praying, will bring revival!

Accept the challenge—pray for national revival, now!

*Let's talk about your "Prayer Meetings."
A good barometer of revival
in your church
is the fervency of your
intercessory prayer meetings.
We must remember that revival
is inseparably linked with prayer
—you cannot have lasting revival
without intercessory prayer.*

—The New Revivalist, 1994.

Chapter 20—Born in a barn

Some of the most wonderful things in the world start small. For instance, the genetic map for a great oak forest is contained in a single little acorn. Even great men, such as Charles Finney, Abraham Lincoln and Martin Luther King Jr., began as tiny fertilized eggs in the wombs of their mothers.

Great revivals also start small, and unbelievably inconspicuous. Consider, for example, the 1949 revival on the Scottish island of Hebrides. Few living on the islands at that time had ever experienced revival. For generations the Church there was dead.

It was then that a young minister, Duncan Campbell, sensing a real need among the young people of his island community, decided to hold revival prayer meetings.

He wanted to hold the prayer meetings outside his church, so he chose a nearby barn. Every Tuesday and Friday nights a small group of intercessors met and prayed for revival, in the barn.

Initially, nothing seemed to happen. The group met faithfully, but not one person was converted during the regular Sunday church services. Campbell did not, however, allow the prayer group to become discouraged. They simply pressed on in faith for revival.

Finally, after three months, the group of intercessors somehow felt that they had prevailed in prayer. Campbell describes a certain "liveliness" taking place in the prayer meetings that had been lacking at first. Convinced that God was about to pour out His Spirit in revival, Campbell announced a special campaign.

However, even though the congregation was greatly moved each night, Campbell did not see a single conversion during the first thirteen days.

It was not until the final night of the special campaign that revival finally broke out. On that fourteenth night, seven young people gave their hearts to God!

After praying with the seven young converts, Campbell delivered the benediction, and the people prepared to go to their homes. However, as the first of the congregation reached the church door, they found the whole community making its way to the church!

"It was as if they were drawn by an unseen hand," Campbell later describes.

So, instead of closing the meeting, Campbell invited them all in, and they really "had church!"

The building was so crowded that Campbell had to seat the visitors on the steps to the altar. For over an hour they all joined in singing hymns and reciting Psalms.

Then, Campbell dismissed the meeting a second time. But, this time he announced that those interested in learning more about God could meet with him in one hour at the home of one of his members, a Mr. McDougall.

Duncan Campbell writes that a huge crowd then packed into McDougall's house, and that many of them were converted that night.

History points to that one service, the last one of the campaign, as the watershed for the Hebrides. That single event ushered in one of the greatest revivals of the twentieth century!

Over the next few years this revival spread throughout all the Hebridean Islands, and then on to Scotland.

All this, from a humble little prayer meeting in a smelly barn!

I believe that when Duncan Campbell first announced to his fledgling congregation that he would be having revival prayer meetings on Tuesday and Friday nights, in a barn, he knew that he could trust God to keep His Word. He knew God would send revival.

Can we, today, trust God *that* much? Has God changed? Does God still keep His promises?

Accept the challenge—pray for national revival, now!

You can read about this and more in: Edwards, Brian H. *Revival, A People Saturated with God.* Durham, England: Evangelical Press (1990) Also, Chapter 31 of *Wind* recounts another interesting event that occurred during the Scottish revival.

Advice to a Young Man – 1884

And then, remember my son, you have to work. Whether you handle a pick or a pen, a wheel-barrow or a set of books, digging ditches or editing a paper, ringing an auction bell or writing funny things, you must work.

If you look around you, son, you will see that the men who are the most able to live the rest of their days without work are the men who worked the hardest. Don't be afraid of killing yourself with work, son. It is beyond your power to do that. Men cannot work so hard as that on the sunny side of thirty. They die sometimes, but it's because they quit work at 6 p.m. and don't get home until 2 a.m. It's the interval that kills, my son.

Work gives you an appetite for your meals, it lends solidity to your slumbers, it gives you a perfect appreciation of a holiday. There are young men who do not work, my son; but the world is not proud of them. It does not even know their names; it simply speaks of them as old so-and-so's boys. Nobody likes them; the great busy world doesn't even know that they are there.

So find out what you want to be, and do it, son, and take off your coat, and make a dust in the world. The busier you are the less deviltry you will be apt to get into, the sweeter will be your sleep, the brighter and happier your holidays, and the better satisfied will the world be with you.

—The Burlington Hawkeye, 1884.

Chapter 21—Personal responsibility

Why do we expect the Federal Government to do everything for us? At what point do we take responsibility for ourselves?

The Church has allowed itself to be sucked into the same "pass the buck" mentality that permeates our whole society. Americans have become obsessed with the notion that the Government should take care of all their problems—if something is not working right, the Government should fix it.

When the family unit first began its rapid decline, rather than repair the broken institution, we chose to pass the responsibility along. At first, we voted to pour more and more money into the school system, in an effort to solve the problem.

When it was obvious that this tactic was failing, we developed the world's biggest welfare system. When it failed, we built bigger and better jails. It was easier to pass that buck than to take responsibility.

It is now estimated that to house all the convicted felons in this nation (approximately 2.3 million), we would have to fence in a facility the size of the five boroughs of New York. Not only does this type of thinking not make sense, it is unbelievable that we wish to continue down that path!

Now that it has become obvious that all of these institutions are unable to solve the family problem, we seek to pass the job one more step up the ladder of Government. "Let the president do it!" We demand. We just need the "right" president.

Get serious, folks, there is no such man out there. No president could do what we are requiring.

It should, therefore, come as no surprise that candidates lie to us. We force an impossible situation upon them, and the weak ones lie. Think about it, a president can't *force* us to act responsibly. It would take more than a dictator to do what we are asking our president to do.

Rather than take personal responsibility, we take ten minutes off, pop into the polling booth, punch the "correct" card, and consider our task complete. We then believe we've done our job in support of family values. The rest is up to the Federal Government.

This type of thinking is irresponsible. Democracy demands responsibility. It does not matter how morally sound an elected leader is, he will never be able to restore our families or the respectability of our land. A president can only reflect such virtues as exist among the people. God, alone, is the healer.

There is only one solution to the problem, according to the Word of God. We need revival. It is exactly that simple. America needs revival. Nothing else can work. The healing has to come from God—it is not the president's job. America needs to get on its face before God and repent.

Not only do sinners need to repent, the Church needs to repent. Remember, it was our job to take the gospel to all the earth. It was our *job*—we were commissioned and commanded. It was not a suggestion—we were *commanded*!

It is our fault that sin is rampant in our country. We cannot blame sinners, we cannot blame the media, MTV, rap music, drug czars or the politicians—we must blame ourselves. It is the direct result of our complacency.

God has already done His part. He has given us all the necessary weapons. The New Testament says that "the weapons of our warfare are not of the flesh, but divinely powerful for the destruction of fortresses" (2 Cor. 10:4). But we just simply choose to sit on the tools He has given us. Could it be we are too lazy?

At similar times during our nation's history (during times of national decline), preachers, lay people, and even businessmen, would look around and decide that they had seen enough, and they cracked open their Bibles.

When they read that God answers prayer, and that 2 Chronicles 7:14 *guarantees* revival, they decided to quit playing church, and start paying the price.

How about you?

Accept the challenge—pray for national revival, now!

God Almighty does not throw dice.

—*Albert Einstein, physicist (author of the
theory of relativity) and Nobel Prize Winner (AGCEQ).*

Chapter 22—Creationists

You have to be pretty stupid to believe in creation, right? Well, that's what secular educators would have us think. But that is not what the real scholars are saying.

In his 1993 book, *Wrinkles in Time* (called by Stephen Hawking "the scientific discovery of all time"), Berkeley cosmologist George Smoot wrote: "My faith is that science will continue to move ever closer to the moment of creation. . . . We are learning that nature is as it is not because it is the chance of consequence of a random series of meaningless events; . . . [it is] as it is because it must be that way."

In his quest for a unified theory, Stephen Hawking seeks to involve everyone in an understanding of the universe: "Then we shall all, philosophers, scientists, and just ordinary people, be able to take part in the discussion of the question of why it is that we and the universe exist . . . for then we would know the mind of God."

Princeton physicist Freeman Dyson wrote in 1988: "The more I study the universe . . . the more evidence I find that the universe in some sense knew we were coming."

Nobel-winning physicist Leon Lederman wrote: "The laws of nature must have existed before even time began in order for the beginning to happen. . . . But can we prove it? No. And what about 'before time began'? Now we have left physics and are in philosophy." This he calls the "God Particle" (*The God Particle,* 1993).

Tulane physicist, Frank Tipler, in his 1994 book: *The Physics of Immortality,* wrote: "This book is a description of the Omega Point Theory, which is a testable physical theory for an omnipresent, omniscient, omnipotent God who will one day in the far future resurrect every single one of us to live forever in an abode which is in all essentials of the Judeo-Christian Heaven."

Although certainly not espousing Christian creationism, still University of Pennsylvania theoretical biologist Stuart Kauffman felt constrained to write these words in 1993: "Natural selection, operating on variations which are random with respect to usefulness, appears a slim force for order in a chaotic world. . . . Our legacy from Darwin, powerful as it is, has fractures as [at?] its foundations."

While I think it is futile to apply the laws of physics or biology to the creator of both, I consider it significant that many of today's top theoretical thinkers are again looking back to an intelligence behind origin.

You should feel intellectually free to accept the challenge, and to pray for national revival. **Now!**

Here are some books by the authors cited above:

Hawking, Stephen W. *A Brief History of Time.* New York: Bantam Books (1988).

Kauffman, Stuart A. *The Origins of Order.* New York: Oxford University Press (1993).

Lederman, Leon. *The God Particle.* New York: Bantam Doubleday Dell Publishing Group, Inc. (1993).

Smoot, George and Davidson, Keay. *Wrinkles in Time.* New York: Avon Books (1993).

Tipler, Frank J. *The Physics of Immortality.* New York: Doubleday (1994).

Chapter 23—The critics of revival

In the 1990s we had a number of "revival outbreaks." First there was "The Laughing Revival;" then "Pensacola;" followed by other centers of revival activity.

During the course of one of those revivals, I read a very critical paper written by a leader of one of the major Pentecostal movements. While its acerbic tone troubled me a bit, it did not surprise me. This type of negativity is to be expected during the early stages of revival.

Over the past years, I have researched thousands of articles and books written by denominational religious leaders during revival movements in America.

I found, for instance, that the Episcopal Church bitterly fought against the Salvation Army. The Lutheran Church opposed the Finney revival. And, almost every denomination of the time battled the Pentecostal movement. It has always been that way: the established churches have always fought against revival. It hasn't changed.

John Wesley made an interesting observation concerning the "excesses" component he saw in earlier revivals. He prayed that God would send another wave of revival to his precious England; but he hoped that this time God would send the new revival without the excesses and weaknesses of the past revivals.

Nevertheless, John Wesley was anxious to accept God's revival, any way God chose to send it; even if it included those dreaded excesses! I think that John Wesley's attitude might serve as an example to guide our efforts today.

I believe that we ought not be unduly distressed with or distracted by revival-like phenomena, such as occurred during the so-called "Laughing Revival" of the 1990s. Instead, with even greater resolve we ought to press on with the hard work of revival: We must get our eyes off others, and totally humble ourselves, surrender our wills, pray with unceasing travailing prayer, repent deeply, fast often, and live lives of total integrity, holiness and soul-winning.

But, before all and above all, we must humble ourselves. All pride must first die.

If we do that, I believe that all the excesses and unbalance will, by themselves, naturally fall away. That's what happened during the times of Whitefield and the Wesley brothers. It happened again and again during the times of Finney, Moody and the Salvation Army. And, it happened that way at Azusa Street, and in Wales. The counterfeit and the weird drop off when the genuine appears.

Negativity is a slippery slope. If we opt to be critical about revival, I believe that we will follow the same path as did the great Episcopal Church during and after the Second Great Awakening. While the Episcopal Church was truly convinced it was defending truth and seeking "genuine" revival, in almost every case its leadership took a very critical stand against revival in general. Rather than do the hard work of revival, it opted to umpire revival's activities. As a result, the great Episcopal Church began a dramatic decline that persists to this day.

I am convinced that many Christians today really do want to see genuine revival. These are the groups and churches which have opened their doors for intercessory prayer meetings, many twenty-four hours a day. That's what they did during the days of Finney, Azusa, and the Welch revival. That's what they do in South Korea.

I believe that when churches resolve to do the hard work of revival, they will have *real* revival. And, once the real exists, the counterfeits and excesses will cease to be attractive, and they will die naturally.

But, until then, I would like to see less criticism. What if this seemingly silly "holy laughter" actually turned out to be an early stage of what God was doing?

I agree with John Wesley. I would like to see God send revival *my* way; but I am willing to let Him do it *His* way!

Accept the challenge—pray for national revival, now!

Students who attended seventeenth century Harvard were not allowed to speak English, even among themselves, and to obtain a degree it was necessary that the candidates should be able to render the Hebrew of the Pentateuch (first five books of the Bible), or the Greek of the New Testament, extempore, into Latin.

—That should not be thought illogical, after all, Harvard was founded as a Bible College.

Chapter 24—Litmus test for revival

Is your church a "religious" church, or a "revival" church? Yes, contrary to some popular thinking, there is a fundamental difference between religion and revival. In fact, the two run in quite different directions. And there is a proven "litmus test" to discriminate between the two.

That being the case, and because churches are primarily outgrowths of one of those two principal driving forces (religion or revival), it then follows that there must also be a fundamental difference between a religious church, and a revival church. Here are some typical distinguishing characteristics:

A religious church often shouts, talks, boasts and devises elaborate plans, with "church growth" as a prominent concept (if not its driving force). A revival church, on the other hand, simply prays.

If carefully examined, a religious church proves to be little more than the codified, petrified relic of a past "move of God"; while a revival church seeks or reflects a fresh "move of God."

A religious church often promotes personalities. Revival churches lift up Jesus. A religious church may seek signs, wonders and gifts. Revival churches seek the Giver of Gifts.

Religion seeks *presents* from a god, revival seeks the *presence* of God.

A religious church may be able to tell you how much money it has in the bank, and how many people it ran in its Sunday services for the past four weeks. And then (without missing a beat) compare those figures with the figures for the same period last year, and the year before. A revival church, on the other hand, can confidently tell you what is the heart of God for that congregation.

A religious church is very concerned with maintaining its non-profit status. Revival churches seek only to please the One who owns the cattle on a thousand hills.

A religious church has more faith in its programs than it has in its God. Revival strives never to quench the Spirit.

Religion, at its heart, is dead. Revival is alive.

"Now," you ask, "exactly how can I tell whether my church is a religious church, or a revival church? What is that litmus test to which you refer?"

First of all, you can't tell a thing by its name. Just because the name of a church is "Revival Cathedral" does not in any sense suggest that it is a revival church. In fact, it has almost become a rule of thumb: If a church has to advertise its revival, it probably doesn't have true revival.

You can't tell by denomination. Many churches founded by old revival movements are now deader than last month's "road pizza."

Neither can you tell by the number of members or by the size of a church's buildings. Large churches can be just as revived, or "unrevived," as smaller ones. Sadly, some prominent churches are purely the product of programs, personalities or promotions—not revival.

So, what is the proven way to distinguish a revival church from a religious church, the so-called "litmus test"?

Simply check the church's bulletin. That's where you will find the revival litmus test. If a church is a revival church, you will find proof in the bulletin.

But, don't look for the word, "revival." Instead, look for a heading such as "Prayer Meeting," or "Intercessory Prayer Meeting."

If a church is well-grounded in the Bible, and if it lists regular prayer meetings in its bulletin, and if those meetings are truly sessions of intense, on-its-face, holiness-seeking, self-effacing, devil-chasing, repentance-hungry, hell-rattling intercessory prayer, then that church either has revival, or is on its way to it.

If, however, that church does not list regular (perhaps daily) congregational intercessory prayer meetings in its bulletin, you can be certain that church is a religious church.

Pay no attention to what it says about itself—you can discount all its promotions and boasting. If a church does not have regular congregational prayer meetings, that church cannot be, neither is it on its way to becoming, a *revival* church.

It is a fact—regular intercessory prayer meetings are the only certain litmus test for a potential revival church.

Accept the challenge—pray for national revival, now!

It cannot be emphasized too strongly or too often that this great nation was founded, not by religionists, but by Christians; not on religions, but on the Gospel of Jesus Christ. For this very reason peoples of other faiths have been afforded asylum, prosperity, and freedom of worship here.

—Patrick Henry, prominent revolutionary. Although offered numerous positions, such as Secretary of State, Chief Justice of the Supreme Court, and Foreign Minister to various countries, he declined them all (AGCEQ).

Chapter 25—Change

Change is the big buzz word today. We are unhappy with the status quo, and we want something different. Exactly *what* we want is unclear. We just know that something is wrong, and we need a change.

As this mood for change sweeps over us here in America, I believe we will react to it in one of two ways. I believe we may just fall on our faces before God, as we have done at various times in our history. If we do this, we will have a revival, and our nation will be healed.

Or, we may seek to implement change only on a human level. We may redouble our attempts to "legislate," "elect," or "enact" some sort of superficial change in a last-ditch effort to save ourselves—sort of like applying a bandage to a bullet wound.

We must be very careful to make the right choice with regard to change. We must not seek change for the sake of change, or change that is strictly of a human agency. The change we seek must be for the face of God, not for the *right* leader, the *right* laws, the *right* economic program, or for the *right* Supreme Court Justices.

Nothing can do the job of a revival. A good, healthy season of revival in America would undo fifty years of neglect. Furthermore, I am convinced that without such a revival, this country will soon not resemble at all the nation we have grown to know, much less the one our Founding Fathers fought to establish.

Without revival, I would not be surprised to see America rapidly implode, and disappear as a viable player on the world stage.

Accept the challenge. Pray daily for national revival. It is, I believe, our only hope. And it is not too late.

*I am much afraid that schools
will prove to be the great gates of hell
unless they diligently labor in explaining
the Holy Scriptures,
engraving them in the hearts of youth.
I advise no one to place his child
where the scriptures do not reign paramount.
Every institution in which men
are not increasingly occupied with the Word of God
must become corrupt.*

—Martin Luther (AGCEQ)

Chapter 26—Repent

T he fellow in Philly looked silly to those who encountered him on the sidewalk, but I think he got it right: "REPENT!"

Not long ago, I spent a day walking through Independence National Historic Park in Philadelphia. I had not been there for twenty-five years. Everything had changed. All the nice signs that gave glory to God were gone. The Christian paintings were gone. The Liberty Bell was no longer on display in Independence Hall. In fact, the entire national library had been removed as well, and disseminated throughout the country. I was greatly disappointed.

One thing was the same, however. The same man that used to walk through the Park a generation ago was still there. He still carried a sign that read:

REPENT
GOD LOVES YOU
BUT HE HATES SIN
DESTRUCTION IS AT HAND

I asked him, "Why do you carry that sign?"

He told me that God had told him to do it. He said that he had done it for years. He used to have a night job, but that now he was retired. This was now his full-time job—ten hours a day, six days a week.

Did he look silly? He sure did. Was his message popular? Not at all—almost everyone laughed at him. Can we criticize his approach? We could. I am sure that there are other ways to get this message out, without that silly sign.

We could certainly question this fellow's good judgment. However, in Jeremiah's day there were certainly those who seriously questioned that prophet's wisdom (if not sanity) for not changing his clothes during all those years. I would guess that Jeremiah's approach was even more radical than that of my friend with the sign.

The bottom line is this: Popularity and acceptance don't impress God. God is not impressed by our great wisdom, or our talent. God isn't worried about whether or not our friends, peers, or our congregations like us.

God doesn't have to take a poll to figure out who's ahead. He knows that even when standing by Himself, He forms an overwhelming majority.

Nope—polls and popularity don't impress God. He is never swayed by public opinion. He never has to campaign for re-election.

What impresses God is submission—our complete submission. In fact, He demands it. God is far more impressed with submission than He is with eloquence, popularity, acceptance or effort.

Even a "foolish" person can be submitted. Was it not God who used one of the submitted foolish things to confound the wise (1 Cor. 1:27)?

I believe that this "foolish" fellow with the sign was right.

While the truth may not be pleasant in the natural, we must all be willing to face it head on.

I believe that the only acceptable solution is for all godly people to put away their sectarian concerns, their reputations, their pride, and to band together on their knees, in agreement, until God sends us national revival.

He has *promised* to do just that! He has promised to send revival if we meet His requirements: "If I shut up the heavens so that there is no rain, or if I command locust to devour the land, or if I send a pestilence among my people, and My people who are called by My name humble themselves and pray and seek My face and turn from their wicked ways, then I will hear from heaven, will forgive their sin and will heal their land" (2 Chron. 7:13-14).

Cotton Mather prayed for four hundred ninety days and nights. The result was the First Great Awakening.

A similar challenge is again before us. If we fail to acknowledge it, or intentionally sidestep it, I believe we will lose our freedom, and our nation.

We, as a nation, must repent. Our national spirit is now overwhelmingly evil. We *must* repent.

The "foolish" fellow in Philly has it right!

Accept the challenge—pray for national revival, now!

We have been the recipients of the choicest bounties of Heaven. We have been preserved these many years in peace and prosperity. We have grown in numbers, wealth and power as no other nation has ever grown.

But we have forgotten God. We have forgotten the gracious Hand which preserved us in peace, and multiplied and enriched and strengthened us; and we have vainly imagined, in the deceitfulness of our hearts, that all these blessings were produced by some superior wisdom and virtue of our own.

Intoxicated with unbroken success, we have become too self-sufficient to feel the necessity of redeeming and preserving grace, too proud to pray to the God that made us!

It behooves us then to humble ourselves before the offended Power, to confess our national sins and to pray for clemency and forgiveness.

—Abraham Lincoln, Sixteenth President of the United States, penned these words in his "Proclamation Appointing a National Fast Day," 1863 (AGCEQ).

Chapter 27—Atlantic Ocean disappears?

D oes this sound like an absurdity? Obviously, there still is an Atlantic Ocean! Isn't there?

This humorous title was suggested by Mr. David Mahorney in a letter to the *Grand Rapids Press* (February 11, 1994). In that letter, Mr. Mahorney suggested that it was ludicrous to think that we are teaching our nation's history while totally ignoring its principal founding document—the Bible.

He further intimated in that letter, that so doing made as much sense as teaching about the exploits of Christopher Columbus or Amerigo Vespucci while denying the "existence of the Atlantic Ocean."

Well, Mr. Mahorney, I am pretty sure that there still is an Atlantic Ocean! But I would totally agree with your concern over the manner in which contemporary "scholarship" treats the teaching of Western Civilization. If, for some reason, the Atlantic Ocean should suddenly become politically incorrect, it could be retroactively declared not to exist. That's how we do things these days in America, in this "enlightened age" of which we boast.

In his letter, Mr. Mahorney alludes to the work of Dr. Donald Lutz (a professor of political science at the University of Houston) to point out how our educational elite distorts the truth.

Mr. Mahorney notes that Dr. Lutz spent a decade researching every recorded quote contained in some fifteen thousand political documents of the Founders' Era (1760-1805).

During the course of his study, Lutz found and analyzed 3,154 citations of the Founders. His work was published in Volume 78 of the *American Political Science Review* (1983).

A statistical analysis of Dr. Lutz's findings clearly refutes contemporary scholarship regarding American History.

Dr. Lutz found that over thirty-three percent of all quotations were directly from the Bible—four times as many as from any other source!

Furthermore, Dr. Lutz found that sixty percent of all the quotations (those quotations not included among the direct quotes from the Bible) were nothing more than ideas derived directly from the Bible!

That could be interpreted to mean that perhaps ninety-four percent of all the ideas that went into our Constitution were based directly or indirectly on the Bible! In 1982 *Newsweek* (December 27) acknowledged that the Bible, even more than the Constitution, served our nation as its "Founding Document."

For our "scholars" to completely ignore the significance of the Bible in the history of America is a travesty to our heritage, and an insult to their profession.

These educators are guilty of nothing less than censorship. This practice is best described as "censorship by omission."

This is the most sinister form of censorship, because it hides behind a facade of false piety. It denies its own existence. It performs its dirty deed in the name of "political correctness."

It certainly is not hard to understand why American youth are testing below every other industrialized nation in the world. When one employs a fraudulent curriculum, one produces fraudulent scholarship.

What's worse, we can claim neither innocence nor ignorance. We were warned that this would happen if we turned our back on the Bible. Benjamin Franklin cautioned us early on concerning this: "I have lived, Sir, a long time and the longer I live, the more convincing proofs I see of this truth—God governs in the affairs of men. And if a sparrow cannot fall to the ground without his notice, is it probable that an empire can rise without his aid? We have been assured, Sir, in the sacred writings that 'except the Lord build they labor in vain that build it.' I firmly believe this; and I also believe that without his concurring aid we shall succeed in this political building no better than the Builders of Babel" (June 28, 1787—AGCEQ).

How did this happen? This falsification of our history did not happen by accident. It occurred as a result of men like John Dewey (commonly regarded as the architect of the American public school system). He wrote: "I cannot understand how any realization of the democratic ideal . . . is possible without the surrender of the basic division to which supernatural Christianity is committed."

I do not think Dewey thought it possible to eliminate religion from American studies without altering history to accomplish it; not in light of Dr. Lutz's findings that ninety-four percent of our Constitution was directly or indirectly based on the Bible. What sort of education schema did Dewey foist on this nation? Obviously, it was one born of deception.

More recently, Paul Blanshard (an influential educator) wrote in *The Humanist* (April, 1976) that "our schools may not teach Johnny to read properly, but the fact that he is in school until the age of sixteen tends towards the elimination of the religious superstition."

The revisionist agenda is clear: rewrite our nation's glorious and godly history in order to eliminate at all cost the recorded influence of religion in its formation—even if it means lying to our children, and "dumbing down" our schools.

Contrary to what our educators are teaching, our Founding Fathers loved the Bible. In fact, the Bible served as our nation's principal founding document—over twenty times as important as all other documents combined!

In 1892, the United States Supreme Court Justices handed down a decision concerning the religious beliefs of our Founding Fathers. They wrote (concerning our nation's heritage): "These, and many other matters which might be noticed, add a volume of unofficial declarations to the mass of organic utterances that this is a Christian nation."

There is simply no *legitimate* counter-argument to be offered—America is a nation founded on the Judeo-Christian ethic. The revisionists have an impossible task if they seek to defend their ideas. It can't be done. Of course, that is not to say that deception cannot be propagated. But if honesty is a player, then this revisionist "house of cards" will eventually have to crumble. After all, perseverance and illumination are immutable qualities of truth.

There is, I believe, a remedy for this situation. Just as it was not too late for a backslidden Israel to turn back to God (2 Chron. 7:14), I am convinced that it is still not too late for us, either.

I am convinced that, as in the day of King Hezekiah, once our ancient books are acknowledged and dusted off, we too will have revival in our land!

Consider this my *official* proclamation: Yes, there truly is an Atlantic Ocean—it really does exist (Mr. David Mahorney was right). Furthermore, let it be known that the Bible also really does exist, and that the study of the Bible is fundamental for an honest understanding of our nation's history.

Education in this nation is an outrage. It is rampant with deception and bad scholarship. We must stop teaching lies.

Accept the challenge—pray for national revival, now! It is truly there for us. In fact, I believe that it will only be in a period of revival that our young people will turn their faces toward the Light of Truth, and away from organized deception.

Chapter 28—A bozo's interpretation of revival

How long has it been since you have read that important Old Testament passage about national revival? It is certainly the most important single Scripture reference concerning national revival. It goes like this:

"If I send pestilence among my people. Sometimes, if I feel like it, when my people, which are called by name, shall humble themselves, and pray, and seek my face, and turn from their wicked ways; then I just might hear from heaven, and review their sin logs, and, if I feel like it, I might consider sending some relief; or maybe not" (2 Chron. 7:13-14 "The Purveyor Interpreter Bible").

"Hey! Just a minute, there," you say, "that's not how *my* Bible reads."

Please, let me explain. Obviously, I have totally changed the words of 2 Chronicles. No matter which ancient Hebrew text I use, I cannot truthfully come up with the above translation.

The above-cited verses actually read: "If . . . My people who are called by My name humble themselves and pray and seek My face and turn from their wicked ways, then I will hear from heaven, will forgive their sin and will heal their land."

I, personally, like the real one better. God certainly has a direct, positive way of expressing Himself, doesn't He? He never feels the need to equivocate. I suppose that's because He's God.

While my butchered rendering of 2 Chronicles seems obvious when considered alongside the correct translation, another similar, but much more subtle error concerning this passage has crept into the church.

This has to do with the popular belief that national revival is strictly the gift of God—sent at His discretion, when He wants to, and only *if* He wants to.

This erroneous thinking holds that man can do little or nothing to bring about revival. The people who support this theory believe that periods of revival are just going to occur at regular times in world history, regardless of the activities of men.

I am convinced that this is not what the Bible says, nor is it what the Bible means. The Bible simply states that God *promises* to send national revival when His people:

1)   Humble themselves

2)   Pray

3)   Seek His (God's) face, and

4)   Turn from their wicked ways.

It is exactly that simple. The NASB (New American Standard Bible) rendering of 2 Chronicles 7:13-14 (cited above) is the correct one—there is absolutely no other correct way to interpret it.

If we follow this directive, God promises to heal our land. It says nothing about Him checking His cosmic watch to see if the next revival train is due.

I believe that this error occurs when people seek God for national revival, and it does not occur right away. It is the result of rationalization: "I prayed, and revival did not come before I finished my cup of coffee. Therefore God must not have meant exactly what He said. Apparently the Revival Express is not yet *due* into the station."

They do this, I believe, so that they will not have to admit that they have failed to do their part. They have wrongfully reinterpreted the Scripture in a very bozo-like manner.

God's promise with regard to revival is as simple as a mathematical equation:

Humility + Prayer + Seeking God + Repentance = National Revival.

It is absolutely, positively not necessary to go beyond this equation to see national revival. God has promised!

We have every right to hold God accountable to His Word. That is exactly what He wants us to do.

Accept the challenge—pray for national revival, now!

*I do not doubt that our country
will finally come through safe and undivided.
But do not misunderstand me. . . . I
do not rely on the patriotism of our people . . .
the bravery and devotions of the boys in blue . . .
(or) the loyalty and skill of our generals. . . .
But the God of our fathers,
Who raised up this country to be the refuge
and asylum of the oppressed and downtrodden
of all nations, will not let it perish now.
I may not live to see it . . .
I do not expect to see it,
but God will bring us through safe.*

—Abraham Lincoln, Sixteenth President of the United States,
penned these words just before the Battle of Gettysburg (AGCEQ).

Chapter 29—The politics of revival

Just before a recent presidential election, I chuckled when I heard my accountant describe the presidential hopefuls as "sailors jumping up and down on the deck of the Titanic (iceberg in sight), frantically waving their hands in the air, and shouting: 'I'll be captain!'"

The last few elections have been different. The issues have become less economic, and more ideological. It seems that everyone senses that there is something deeply significant happening in this nation—something that somehow makes recent elections more impacting than those in the past. Talking heads on both sides of the aisle are going a little nuts.

While I do agree that these are terribly significant days in American political history, and that current elections are extremely important, I do have a problem with assuming that we Christians necessarily know the mind of God in choosing the "right" president for this country, for this time.

The Bible says that God (not man) raises leaders up, and brings them down. In the book of Jeremiah, God refers to King Nebuchadnezzar as "His servant," overlooking completely Judah's king, Zedekiah.

It is interesting that God looked outside Judah for "His Servant." Don't you think that He could have found one righteous candidate in the nation of Judah? Jeremiah lived there, you know. Why not raise Jeremiah up to be king? Could it be that God knew that the people would not follow Jeremiah?

Even though the Babylonian's appointed role was a destructive one (to bring down and into captivity the idolatrous nation of Judah), God still referred to King Nebuchadnezzar as *His* servant. Nebuchadnezzar was obviously the right man in God's eyes, for that time.

Why did God do it this way? I would offer this theory: God knew that His people needed to repent more than anything else in the world, and He brought about a situation conducive to repentance. It is that simple, I believe.

At that time in history the people of Judah were terribly evil—they wanted no part of God or His laws. Jeremiah knew it, and he proclaimed it loud and clear to the people, and to King Zedekiah. Interestingly, Zedekiah did not dispute Jeremiah's prophecy at all. In fact, in a passive way, he accepted it. We know that he accepted it because he did not put Jeremiah to death, as was the custom—he actually protected Jeremiah from the people.

However, sparing His prophet was not enough to suit God—Judah needed a *national* revival. Nothing else would do the job. Zedekiah, being a weak man, was unwilling to pay the price for revival, and he knew that he was impotent to "fix" the problem by decree, so he ignored it. It cost him and his family their lives, and Judah its freedom.

We can easily relate this story to American presidential elections, and our desire to find the "right" man to heal our land.

I think we are seriously mistaken if we think that any presidential candidate, once elected, would (or could) do much of anything to solve America's problems. Even though some of the candidates might themselves possess outstanding morals and family values, they cannot mandate righteousness.

It is impossible to legislate true morality in any society, especially a free society—it always has been this way. Our leaders can appoint Supreme Court Justices, but they will never be able to legislate family values, any more than our government was able to make prohibition work.

Elected leaders are nothing more or less than a representation of the corporate mind-set. Under our form of government, righteous voters produce righteous government, not the other way around.

Furthermore, I am completely convinced that it is nothing less than a corporate "wimp-out" for the Church to push the responsibility for dealing with the disgusting state of the family in America onto the Government's shoulders.

We must realize that the real battle will never be fought in the voting booth. We must also realize that the real enemy is not drugs, crime, or any of the other filthy vices that plague us. These are only symptoms of the disease—the real disease is sin. Our real battle will never be against flesh and blood, but against spiritual forces of wickedness (Eph. 6:12).

What are the weapons of our warfare? The Bible makes it clear that God has already given us all the necessary weapons for this battle. They are powerful weapons. The Bible lists these weapons for us—most of us have read about them, so we may all know what they are. If these weapons are used, they will bring down strongholds—that's the purpose for which they were designed. They will not fail us. God will not fail us.

Even our Founding Fathers recognized where and how this battle was to be fought, and how God's weapons were to be used. It was commonplace for presidents such as Washington, Monroe, Adams, and even Abraham Lincoln, to call for national days of fasting and prayer.

That is exactly what we need to do. This battle will be fought with fasting and prayer, on our faces before God. We must confess and repent of all sins, ask forgiveness from God, and from those we've wronged. Then, we must seek God's presence. If we do that, God will keep his promise. He will heal our land. It is very, very simple—not *easy*, but very simple.

In the end, it will all come down to whether or not we are serious about doing battle. Whether we like it or not, just as it is in athletic events, the "wimp factor" (temptation to give up when fatigue sets in) will threaten success.

It will come down to a question of willpower, not firepower. If we truly want victory, we will go to war the way God taught us. We will do battle as though everything depended upon it—because it does.

When we get serious about solving our problems today (serious enough to quit passing the buck), we will bend our stiff necks and get on our faces before Almighty God, and cry out to Him. When we do this, He will hear us, forgive us, and heal our land—it is no more difficult than that. He has promised, and He is faithful.

Our *seeking*, however, must be for the face of God, not for the "right" president. King Zedekiah could do no more than wring his hands and bite his nails at the prophecy of Jeremiah, even though he accepted it. He could not mandate righteousness in his country, and he wasn't willing to pay the price for revival.

Just as the King of Judah was unable to save his people, so is an elected American president impotent to mandate righteousness in America. If righteous leadership would make a nation righteous, why did they hang Jesus on a tree?

I would invite you to look around—take a very close look. Then, ask yourself, "Is this what I want? Do I approve of family deterioration, drive-by killings, illicit drug use, crime, perversions of every sort (including religious perversions), suicide and apathy?"

If, then, you are satisfied with what you see (if you think life in America is pretty much okay), forget everything I have written—you are obviously happy. Go back into your closet and match up your suits and ties, skirts and tops. Don't worry about a thing.

But, if you are absolutely sickened by what you see around you, and if you don't want to pass the buck any more; then maybe you are ready to get serious about fixing it.

You are deluding yourself if you think that you are going to solve the problem by giving it to the President. It doesn't matter how upright that man is, he is only a man. Our land needs a revival more than a new president. Without revival our land will fall. It is exactly that clear. It should be a no-brainer.

I believe that it would be the greatest of all modern-day tragedies if the Church rallies around some political candidate thinking that this man, or that man, can "save" America for righteousness.

In fact, if our goal is totally political, and we are able to elect those "right" candidates (whoever we think they are), we will be left with an even worse situation than we now face, because our "victory" will be false—it will be a "placebo," a sugar tablet. True victory will come only with revival.

Where does such a revival come from? Is it something that God periodically sends upon His people, like a warm cozy blanket? That is not the case at all.

God tells us that revival will come only when His people humble themselves, confess their sins, and seek His face. Only then will He hear from heaven, forgive their sins, and heal their land. We must do our part to start the revival. To think otherwise is bad theology, or laziness—probably both.

We must remember: No elected officials can make this happen for us. You and I alone can make it happen.

Accept the challenge—pray for national revival, now!

If [Congress] be ignorant, reckless, and corrupt,
it is because the people tolerate ignorance,
recklessness and corruption. If it be intelligent,
brave, and pure,
it is because the people demand these high qualities
to represent them in the national legislature.

—James Garfield, twentieth President of the United States (AGCEQ).

Chapter 30—Hey, Teach, are you absolutely certain there are no absolutes?

A t most colleges and universities, a professor greets his incoming freshmen with a declaration much like this: "Forget about God, forget about ultimate truth, or ultimate truths, dispense with all preconceptions. Know only one thing—there are *no* absolutes."

With that statement, and a haughty elevation of an eyebrow, the professor begins his attack on the young minds' value systems.

"Forget whatever Daddy and Mommy told you about God, truth, and values," the professor demands. "Each person must develop his own system of understanding as to what truth is to him."

"Truth," continues Professor Pompus Longnose, "is relative. My truth is not necessarily your truth; but both truths may still be true. You must understand, and come to appreciate the fact, that truth is subjective."

Theoretically, this approach is designed to enlarge the young mind and force it to re-think and update its value system.

There is no doubt that it has accomplished its purpose—the minds of the students are definitely expanded; many to the point of cranial obesity.

Unfortunately, along with everything else that the young are discarding, they are turning their backs on the very cohesive force that has for over two centuries held our culture together—God. By removing God, our educational philosophy is causing this nation to disintegrate.

What happens when truth is relative? We have found that when biblical truths are yanked out of the mind of a man such as John Wayne Gacy, anything goes, even serial killing.

One jury's version of "truth" accepted the Menendez brothers' excuse for killing their parents. The "truth" believed by six policemen allowed them to beat Rodney King senseless. A similar subjective truth explains how it was okay to smash truck driver Denny over the head with a brick and a wine bottle.

The problem is that once truth becomes relative, we can no longer function as an orderly free society. Without absolutes, such as truth, we cannot even begin to govern ourselves appropriately.

Forget about what the Constitution says. Forget what the laws on the books say. All we have to do to find out today's truth is to take a poll and see what the current public opinion says about any given issue.

This phenomenon makes it very easy to create new truths. To do this, we first take out a full-page ad in the *New York Times* and in the *LA Times,* promoting whatever we wish to promote. Then, three days later, we take a public-opinion poll. Even foreign interests can (and do) participate in this practice.

If we fall a little short of a majority, we simply repeat the procedure until we are successful. Of course, once we have established this new "truth," we stop taking polls. And, it goes without saying, it never hurts to toss in a couple celebrity endorsements along the way. We all know how brilliant and outspoken these folks are.

The media is more than a tool in these types of endeavors—they are very willing participants. This is particularly true of the news media. Once the job of journalists was to dig up the facts and objectively report the news on the basis of those facts. Today many "journalists" admit to having entered the field "to make a difference." That is not real reporting.

It is a simple fact that our "wise men" have outsmarted themselves with their designer truths. Our society is not evolving to a "higher level of existence," as it contends. Any fool with blinders on can see that our value-less society, so highly esteemed by our intellectual elite, is actually destroying our nation.

The Bible says that "The fear of the Lord is the beginning of wisdom, And the knowledge of the Holy One is understanding" (Prov. 9:10f).

It also says: "Behold, the fear of the Lord, that is wisdom; and to depart from evil is understanding" (Job 28:28); that "Revive me, O Lord, according to Your lovingkindness. The sum of Your word is truth, And every one of Your righteous ordinances is everlasting" (Ps. 119:159b-160); and that "Let God be found true, though every man be found a liar, as it is written, 'That You may be justified in Your words, And prevail when You are judged'" (Rom. 3:4).

"For even though they knew God, they did not honor Him as God or give thanks, but they became futile in their speculations, and their foolish heart was darkened. Professing to be wise, they became fools . . . Therefore God gave them over in the lusts of their hearts to impurity . . . For they exchanged the truth of God for a lie" (Rom. 1:21-25).

Oh, you foolish professors, how can you be absolutely sure there are no absolutes?

I have thought about this a great deal, and I am absolutely certain that only the power of God in national revival can put an end to this folly, and turn this nation around.

Accept the challenge—pray for national revival, now!

O God, we have heard with our ears,
Our fathers have told us
The work that You did in their days,
In the days of old.
You with Your own hand drove out the nations;
Then You planted them; . . .
For by their own sword they did not possess the land,
And their own arm did not save them,
But Your right hand and Your arm
and the light of Your presence,
For You favored them.

—Psalms 44:1-3.

Chapter 31—Saturated with God

(Much of this account of the Campbell prayer meeting, and the Edwards' quote, can be found in a book by Brian H. Edwards, *Revival, A People Saturated with God*. Durham, England: Evangelical Press (1990); and in the published account of the Campbell revival available online at http://www.revival-library.org/pensketches/revivals/hebrides.html.)

It started out as a normal week-night prayer meeting. There had been some opposition to the gospel in the area, and a general sense of apathy seemed to prevail. Although many attended the meetings from other areas, very few locals were there.

Prayer, this night, was unusually difficult. The intercessors persisted throughout the evening and into the night, but without the sense that they had "prayed through."

About midnight, Duncan Campbell (the prayer leader) turned to the local blacksmith, who had been silent so far, and said: "John, I feel that God would have me to call upon you to pray."

It was always difficult for the old man to pray, for his nature was that of a very quite and private person.

Nevertheless, once he got started praying, the rough blacksmith prayed for about half an hour.

As the old man was about to draw his prayer to a close, he felt constrained to halt, and to listen for the voice of God. He just stood there silently for a few moments. Then, the Spirit of God led him to end his prayer with this bold challenge:

"God, do you not know that your honor is at stake? You promised to pour floods on dry ground, and you are not doing it."

He paused again for a moment, and then concluded: "God, your honor is at stake, and I challenge you to keep your covenant engagements."

At that moment, the whole granite building in which they were praying shook like a leaf, and while one elder thought it an earth tremor, Duncan Campbell was reminded of Acts 4:31: "And when they had prayed, the place where they had gathered together was shaken."

It was, by then, about two o'clock in the morning. Duncan Campbell pronounced the benediction, and the intercessors ventured outside to see what was happening. They found the whole village "ablaze with God." Men and women were carrying chairs and asking if there was room in the church for them!

What, then, is revival? According to Duncan Campbell, revival is a "people saturated with God."

"In revival," writes Brian Edwards, "things happen suddenly and unexpectedly. Meetings are lengthened, crowds gather, and sermons have to be preached, not because it is all arranged in advance, but because God is at work.

"People will arrive without warning for a meeting, moved by an unseen hand. Isaiah described such a time when God did 'awesome things which we did not expect, You came down, the mountains quaked at Your presence' (Isa. 64:3).

"In revival God takes over, . . . all the elements [in revival] are present in the normal life of the church, . . . but in revival they are heightened and intensified. . . . The main difference between the normal life of the church and revival is that in revival you find the old things with new life."

I like that. People, more than things, are changed in revival—because new wine won't be contained in old wine skins (Matt. 9:17).

My prayer is this: "O, God, please revive your people again. Change us. Make us a people saturated with Your Spirit. May Your people pray with unceasing, unrelenting power. May they start today."

Accept the challenge—pray for national revival, now!

Chapter 32—When is a revival meeting not a revival meeting?

Not all revival meetings are actually revival meetings. If someone tells you that their church called for a One-Week Revival Prayer Emphasis last month, and if there is no evidence of revival, they did not have a *true* revival prayer meeting.

The fact is that any so-called "revival" prayer meetings (or series of lectures or seminars) that call upon God for revival, but only for a set period of time, are worse than useless—they are counter-productive. If anyone announces a one-time "Revival Prayer Meeting," he is misrepresenting his meeting—it's not an actual revival prayer meeting.

If I tell you that I am having three weeks of revival prayer, what I am really saying is, "I don't believe for a minute that God is going to send revival, but I am willing to bend my knee for a few weeks to relieve tension." It would indicate that I have no intention of humbling myself, and that I do not intend to really repent.

Does this make you uncomfortable? Perhaps you are thinking that right about now might be a good time to stop reading my book. Maybe your phone is about to ring. Or, maybe you are starting to get thirsty. This might even be a very good time to go to the grocery store.

Don't worry. It is okay to be uncomfortable. The truth doesn't have to feel good. If, however, you are strong enough to handle the truth, bite down hard on your pencil, and I'll continue. If you follow along, you will see that there is a huge price to pay if you are going to be the intercessor that God is looking for. If you think you might be up to the challenge, I'll lay it out for you.

My friend, I declare to you that an intercessor can know only two postures: on his knees seeking revival, or basking in one.

Furthermore, I declare that it is impossible to have true revival meetings, without experiencing subsequent revival. Meetings come and go, but they are not real revival meetings unless they are on-going; or, unless revival follows them. We have not truly prayed for revival unless we are presently living in revival, or continuing to pray for it EVERY DAY, WITHOUT FAIL.

It doesn't matter what we call it. If it is not on-going and unrelenting, it is not true revival prayer.

God's promise for national revival remains very simple: "If . . . My people who are called by My name humble themselves and pray and seek My face and turn from their wicked ways, then I will hear from heaven, and will forgive their sin and will heal their land" (2 Chron. 7:13-14).

This promise is very straightforward. It requires no special interpretation. That's exactly how history has viewed this passage. In fact, every great national revival has regarded the literal interpretation of 2 Chronicles 7:14 as the single most important promise concerning the hand of God on a nation.

It is exactly that simple. The literal interpretation of 2 Chronicles 7:13-14 is the right one—there is absolutely no other correct way to interpret it.

That's the challenge. God is able. God does not lie. God has promised. If we want revival, we must do our part.

YES, WE CAN HAVE NATIONAL REVIVAL! AND WE CAN HAVE IT AS SOON AS WE ARE READY FOR IT!

Accept the challenge—pray for national revival, now!

Chapter 33—The incredible inconvenience of revival

D o we really have time for revival? This question is actually more valid than it might appear on the surface. I believe that it raises an issue that deserves serious consideration.

A few months into my fasting and prayer, a close friend offered me what he perceived to be a "reality pill"—figuratively speaking.

What my friend did was confront me with a practical fact about revival (howbeit, one that had virtually escaped my attention).

Having just finished reading one of my articles on revival, my friend asked me if I was really serious about attending church five days a week, perhaps eight or ten hours a day.

"Frequently, during revival," he pointed out, "the meetings would last for days and even weeks, without even the hint of stopping. How will you work to support your family, if you are in church all day?"

He had a point. He was right about revival. Historically, revivals consumed an enormous amount of a participant's time. Anyone who became fully involved with a revival had to expect to spend a very large part of his time doing those things demanded by the revival.

In one case, a powerful revival service started on a Sunday morning, continued throughout the week, and ended on the following Friday morning. People would come and go, but the service continued without a letup (Methodist Revival, Tuckingmill in Cornwall, 1814).

During the Azusa movement, church doors remained open twenty-four hours a day, seven days a week, for three years!

My friend's question definitely caught me off guard, and truly got me thinking.

I did not have a good answer for him, at that time. I was simply not sure how I would cope with the seemingly incredible inconvenience of revival. After acknowledging my weakness in this area, I prayed and asked God to give me His wisdom to answer my friend, with both conviction and love.

I believe God answered my prayer. It came to my mind that the question raised by my friend was very much like the old skeptic's criticism of heaven.

"Who," the skeptic asks rhetorically, "would ever want to go to heaven just to sit around playing a harp for eternity?"

The answer the skeptic seeks is: "No thinking person would ever want to subject himself to such boredom."

However, the correct answer to the question is: "Heaven is not to be desired because of what we will do there; heaven is desirable because of Whom we will experience there!"

In just the same way, the glory of revival is found in the overwhelming presence of our God, not in the length or frequency of church meetings!

Think about it! In past revivals no one had to twist arms to get the people to pray and to worship for days, weeks, and even months. There were no armed guards preventing people from leaving!

People willingly flocked to the meetings because they encountered God there! To the "unrevived" (and right now that term can be rightly applied to virtually the whole Church in America), this concept is very difficult to understand, much less to appreciate.

Think about it. These old-time revivalists did not even have air-conditioning! In the natural, this seems stupid!

I am convinced that the only bonding agent that could have glued these people together during those hot, smelly church and tent services, for days and weeks on end, was the mighty presence of the God of Heaven and Earth.

I now stand convinced that it was the overwhelming, saturating Spirit of the Living God that held those revival meetings together. He is the One around whom the revivals happened. The hard work of the facilitators brought it about, but it was the presence of the Living God that made those facilitators forget about their discomforts.

So, I now have an answer for my friend: "Yes, I want revival! I want more of God, no matter what the cost! I long to be totally saturated with Him! While I cannot imagine, right now, how my busy life will accommodate it, I am confident that God will work it out, somehow."

My prayer now is: "O God, send revival to your church; send revival to me. I don't care what it looks like. Do it anyway You choose. I don't even care how You 'inconvenience' me with it. But, please, O God, don't leave me on the river bank when Your revival waters flow."

I now better understand what God wants me to do. I now welcome and invite "the inconvenience of revival."

Accept the challenge with me—pray for national revival, now!

The highest level to which man can aspire in his walk with God is to be God's own "pocket change."
God's own personal discretionary money, available as needed, and ready to be spent.

—*The Rev. M. Wayne Benson.*

Chapter 34—Who was the dumbest stump in the Bible?

That sure doesn't sound very complimentary. Surely, no one would ever want to be known as the dumbest stump in the Bible.

But there was one prominent figure in the Bible who admitted to be being dumb—really dumb; perhaps even dumber than Forrest Gump. Can you guess who that was?

I think the answer will surprise you. The dumb guy was Paul the Apostle. Don't you find that a little surprising?

It is true, of course, that Paul was a very learned man. He had studied at the feet of some of the chief scholars, such as Gamaliel. And Gamaliel was known as one of the greatest intellectuals of the time. However, Paul preferred ignorance over brilliance. It was his choice.

He wrote: "And when I came to you, brethren, I did not come with superiority of speech or of wisdom, proclaiming to you the testimony of God. For I determined to know nothing among you except Jesus Christ, and Him crucified.... My message and my preaching were not in persuasive words of wisdom, but in demonstration of the Spirit and of power, so that your faith would not rest on the wisdom of men, but on the power of God" (2 Cor. 2:1ff).

So, it is true, Paul was a dumb stump. What is even more amazing is that he was stump dumb by choice! He *chose* to know nothing except Jesus and the Crucifixion.

Why would a man with Paul's intellectual abilities approach evangelism using the Forrest Gump methodology of "dumbness"?

I believe that Paul wisely opted for the most direct and effective approach available to him. Paul simply knew that a man with an experience is never at the mercy of a man with an argument, no matter how strong and compelling that argument might be. I'll give you an example of how this works:

Mr. Dumb says: "I just finished my Luscious Chocolate Bar. Boy was it good!"

Mr. Too Smart counters: "Did you say you *finished* your Luscious Chocolate Bar? I don't think so, Mr. Dumb, because that's quite impossible! You could not possibly have eaten the *whole* Luscious Chocolate Bar. And I can prove it!

"You see, Mr. Dumb, before you could have finished the Luscious Chocolate Bar, you must first have eaten half of it. Then, once you have eaten half, you must then eat half of the remaining half. And, of course, then half of that remaining half, then half of that; etc., etc.

"Don't you understand, Mr. Dumb, this process of division must logically take place an infinite number of times, thus making the task of ever actually *completing* the Luscious Chocolate Bar a mathematical impossibility!"

To this, Mr. Dumb responds: "Sorry, Mr. Too Smart, I truly did eat the whole Luscious Chocolate Bar! And, I really enjoyed it! See, here's the empty wrapper! Check it out!

"Besides, Mr. Too Smart, if I didn't actually eat the *whole* Luscious Chocolate Bar, where is it? I can show you the empty wrapper, you show me the Luscious Chocolate Bar!"

Folks, that's all God asks of us. He wants us to be dumb stumps like Paul. He wants us to be radically obedient, not intellectually superior.

He wants us to do the Great Commission, not merely describe it.

He wants us to tell people what He has done in our lives, not cleverly expound upon all the great theological niceties of our faith.

All the wisdom of the world cannot convince Mr. Dumb that he did not really eat the whole Luscious Chocolate Bar—he knows beyond a shadow of a doubt that he ate the whole thing.

If you know Jesus, all the wisdom of the world cannot convince you otherwise. Just tell people what He has done in your life—that's all Jesus asks you to do.

You will discover that all the "Yeah Buts" in the world cannot refute your testimony, because your personal *experience* can never be challenged by another's *argument*, no matter how vociferously propounded, and no matter how compelling.

God is looking for a few good dumb stumps. If you can still fog a mirror, you can be one!

Accept the challenge—pray for national revival, now!

The following questions were commonly discussed by candidates for degrees from Harvard University, 1655-1791 (in the Latin tongue, of course):

Is agriculture unbecoming a gentleman?

Is there a stone that makes gold?

Was there a rainbow before the deluge?

Did reptiles of America originate from those that were preserved by Noah?

Were Samson's foxes, as they are commonly called, animals?

When the shadow went back on the sun-dial of Hezekiah, did the shadows go back upon all sun-dials?

And, did Jacob's opposition to his wife while she was dying, in calling his son Benjamin, when she had previously named him Benoni, proceed more from his determination to exercise his authority as a husband than from his petulant disposition?

—Standard of the Cross, 1880.

Chapter 35—Bend the Church, save the people

Why is revival flourishing around the world, yet still faltering in America? I think I know at least one of the reasons.

Recently (when this chapter was first written) a young couple addressed our Wednesday night Bible Study. They had just completed a tour to Albania with an itinerant choir and orchestra. They explained that for decades Albanian Christians had been killed or imprisoned, resulting in the dissolution of any established church there.

"But now," they said, "that policy was changing."

The couple also reported that immediately upon landing in Albania their group asked for and received permission to hold a concert. They set up their seventeen-piece orchestra in front of their hotel, and performed totally impromptu. Five thousand Albanians stopped to hear them.

As is typical after this group's concert, members gave their personal testimonies. At this concert these testimonies were translated by an atheist Albanian national. He had been commissioned by the government to accompany the group.

After the testimonies, an "altar call" was given, again by this same atheist. After the altar call, every single person in the audience acknowledged his need for God, and subsequently gave his heart to Jesus Christ— five thousand heard the Word, five thousand accepted it.

By the time the group boarded their plane to leave Albania a few days later, twenty thousand had accepted Jesus as Lord, a church had been planted with six hundred members, and the atheist translator got saved!

I wept when I heard this report. Long after my class was dismissed, I remained. It pierced my heart to see how free God was to move on the hearts of the Albanians, while in America we continue to resist Him with white-knuckled stubbornness.

I think that we in America have become so wise in our own eyes we think we don't need God. We know so much about the Word of God we can argue it with anybody—and we do. We pride ourselves more in our knowledge of the Bible than in our relationship with its author. "Woe to you, scribes and Pharisees, hypocrites, because you devour widows' houses, and for a pretense you make long prayers; therefore you will receive greater condemnation" (Matt. 23:14).

Fortunately, when these twenty thousand Albanians got saved there were no self-righteous Christian skeptics standing back telling them they were "doing it wrong."

The time has come for Americans to do 2 Chronicles 7:14.

Let us humble ourselves, now. Let us learn a lesson from the Albanians. Let us have revival in *our* land!

"Bend the Church to save the people" was the motto of Revivalist Evan Roberts during the great Welsh Revival of 1904.

I say it's time to bend the Church in this country.

Accept the challenge—pray for national revival, now!

Chapter 36—Is anyone seeking revival today?

I do believe that there are a number of people in this nation who are truly seeking for national revival. For years these intercessors have cried out to God, hour after hour, day after day, year after year. Their cry: "Do it again! O God, send revival, again—nation-changing revival, as in the day of Charles Finney."

In 1995 I talked with such a man—an old-time retired preacher, I think he was almost ninety years old at that time. It was at the same campground that I visited weekly for fasting and prayer, and it was also where he lived. He was taking his morning exercise walk. He stopped for a moment to talk with me. His eyes were like steel. They seemed to focus somewhere beyond my eyes, perhaps deep into my spirit, or even beyond.

He staggered slightly as he talked, sometimes totally losing his balance for a moment. "I'm getting tired," he said, looking worried. "My body just gets so tired these days. But," he continued, "we must, we *must*, have a revival. Not revival in a building, or even a city, but across the whole country. We must have a *real* revival, one sent from God. One that no man can take credit for. But, I get so tired now, when I pray."

He looked at me even more deeply, and said, "I'm going home soon. My body will not hold out much longer. It is getting harder and harder for me to pray. I get so tired."

His focus changed suddenly. It was as though he finally looked at me and saw my flesh, and realized what his life was truly about. I was a mere mortal. Perhaps he thought I couldn't understand. Or, perhaps he thought that I might patronize him.

At any rate, he squeezed out a quick smile, turned, and hobbled away toward his cottage. He never said a word as he left, not even a goodbye.

I don't think that he wanted to hear any more shallow promises. Many in the state of Michigan had known for years of his great burden for revival. And I'm sure he had heard all the half-hearted excuses. Now, with his pastoring days over, his business was with God alone, for whatever time he had left.

It was obvious he was finished talking to me. I stood in my tracks for just a moment to watch that old saint cut through the forest towards his home.

I then turned, and headed for my prayer closet. My eyes glazed over before I reached my door, and tears were streaming off my chin before my knees hit the floor. I cannot remember having cried so much in my life.

I later left that room with a surety in my soul. I will even be bold enough to pass it on, as a *promise* to you. Without a single doubt in my mind, I guarantee that we will have national revival. God is preparing His people for it right now! Intercessors like this saint have laid the foundation. God will honor His Word. He has promised.

This saintly old friend of mine has now gone to be with his God. He never got to see the revival for which he so earnestly sought the last years of his life—at least not through his earthly eyes.

I was not there when he passed on, but I would not be surprised if revival was on his mind as he left. As far as this godly man was concerned, there were only two ways to live—seeking revival, or basking in it.

I implore you to join hearts with this old saint, the Reverend Parvin Lee, and with me.

Accept the challenge—pray for national revival, now!

Chapter 37—Ready for a challenge?

I believe that the Church is beginning to wake up! In fact, I believe that a great revival has already begun!

How would you like to be a part of it? You can, you know! Here's the challenge:

• Form a group of five or six friends to get together with you for prayer and testimonies once each week, for as long as it takes.

• Do not serve refreshments at (or after) these meetings.

• Each member of your group must agree to spend thirty minutes (alone) every morning in prayer and Bible study; to write down daily what truth he got from the Word; to share his faith once each day; and to give a testimony at the weekly meeting with the group.

• At the end of sixty days, each of the original six members must then pick five other friends and begin holding meetings with them. It is critical that these prayer meetings never become social gatherings or fellowship groups.

• At the end of each sixty-day cycle, all groups should again divide.

• Additional prayer times, such as "all-night prayer meetings," may be held as God leads; but they must not take the place of the weekly group prayer meeting.

What should you expect this challenge to produce? That's impossible to predict. However, in one instance it facilitated a wonderful revival.

In October of 1969, a single young college girl did exactly as I have outlined above. She had a tremendous hunger for revival at her college, so she sought out five like-minded students who would share her burden.

By January of 1970, the original group had divided into six groups of six, or thirty-six young people.

The president of the college had heard about the group, and he asked them to address the student body at a chapel service.

This group of thirty-six students stood before their fellow college students on Tuesday, January 31, and shared what God was doing in their lives. They then challenged the whole student body to become part of a group of six who would agree to pray for thirty days.

The next chapel service was scheduled for February 3 (one week later). The dean was supposed to speak. Instead, he gave only a short testimony, and then invited students to do the same.

The power of God fell on that assembly like a nuclear explosion. For one full week, day and night, the students remained at that altar, crying out to God in repentance.

This visitation from God, which came to be known as "The Asbury Revival," was carried by students from that small Kentucky campus, and repeated throughout the nation, resulting in tens of thousands of changed lives.

Could it happen again?

It sure could! And it could even be much more powerful than it was in the previous instance. Just imagine what would happen if you and your friends committed to prayer just as those young students committed to prayer.

That's the challenge. Are you up to it?

If so, begin praying for national revival, now.

Chapter 38—Fasting and prayer: the ultimate excitement?

I believe that fasting and prayer produces the greatest excitement attainable in this life. In fact, I believe that fasting and prayer is the single most exhilarating thing that a human being can do. I mean that. It is truly exciting. I am convinced that fasting and prayer beats anything else that I have ever done, or can even think of! I have received a higher high during times of fasting and prayer than I have skydiving.

If you snicker a little at this thought; then, I suggest, you have not really learned how to do it. At least, you have not learned how to do it right.

You see, there is a right and wrong way to fast and pray.

Jesus fasted, you know. He fasted for forty days. I can't imagine that—forty days. To fast like that would be terribly difficult (if not impossible) if you didn't do it right. I am sure Jesus did it right.

In fact, fasting for even one day can be very hard, if you don't do it right. I know, because I used to do it the wrong way. Believe me, there is nothing exciting about this exercise when you do it wrong.

My mistake was that I would try to work on fast days. I found that I was not accomplishing a thing. I would just get nervous and hostile. I really didn't get anywhere with God—I simply got terribly hungry, and miserably cantankerous.

I got started fasting when my pastor called for a fast on Tuesdays. Then, when that period of fasting ended, I decided to continue fasting on Tuesdays.

At that time, it was not fun at all. But, I figured that since Jesus did it, and the disciples did it, I should give it a try. Yet, even though it seemed like the proper thing to do, I hated it—every minute of it.

The worst thing about it was that I was making everyone around me very unhappy—my wife included. I couldn't help it. Someone would walk up to me with a question, and I'd bite his head off: "What do you mean, 'It's time for lunch.' We just got started. We can eat later. Let's just get this job done!"

I was a bear! If I couldn't eat, I didn't want anyone else to eat—especially in front of me. In fact, I practically required those around me to have written permission to breathe!

I decided that if I was going to continue fasting, I would have to find a better way.

With a little encouragement from my wife, I decided to try something new, for one Tuesday—I would spend the day away from the human race, and away from food.

It wasn't easy to find a place where I could be alone. That's when I started going to our house trailer on the lake. There I could escape phone calls, doorbells, and all other distractions. As I anticipated my first trip to the trailer, my only concern was about my next-door neighbor at the campground—my brother, Jack.

Usually, whenever I went to the lake, I would look forward to spending a lot of time with my brother. It was about the only time we ever got to see each other. However, I knew that if I was fasting, and he came around, I would probably just bite his head off. That could start a family feud.

I called him the day before, and warned him that I was going to come up to the trailer to fast and pray the next day.

I confidently informed him that I would be busy praying until about 5 p.m. or so. After that, we could go out for dinner, or do whatever he might suggest. Actually, I had no idea how long it would take to fast and pray. I thought 5 p.m. sounded about right. I really didn't know what to expect.

Now, you have got to know my brother Jack to appreciate my concern. Jack is an old-time retired preacher—he is absolutely *impossible* to ignore. He's a totally beautiful person, but very outgoing. He's a little like a nervous puppy—he won't quit jumping on you until you notice him. I love him to death.

However, I could just picture him running around the trailer, moving this or that, raking leaves, moving stones, planting trees, digging up trees, or washing windows. I just knew that he would do something to get my attention, and break my concentration.

I did not want to be disturbed, not even by my much-loved brother. After all, I was "fasting and praying"—whatever *that* really meant.

When I arrived at the campground, I at first looked around to see where my brother was. His car was gone, so I assumed that he and Mary (my sister-in-law) went out for breakfast.

"Good," I thought, "I won't have to explain this business to anyone! Today I am really going to find out what it is to fast and pray."

All during the drive from Grand Rapids to Jackson I had listened to a cassette tape entitled, *Practicing the Presence of God.* I was anticipating a real encounter with God—how it was to take place, or what it was to be like, I didn't have the foggiest notion.

I did know, however, that I did not want to be disturbed, by anyone. This was going to be between me and God. I was going to be like George Washington and Abraham Lincoln, at least for one day.

I parked my car across from the trailer, scooped up my Bible and a couple of other books, and headed across the drive—undetected. I opened the screen door, and reached into my pocket for the trailer key.

Not finding the key in my pocket, I set my bundle down, so that I might check my other pockets. I then remembered that, in my rush to sneak in, I had left the trailer key in the car.

Back across the drive I scurried to get the key. I quickly snatched it out of the glove box, and darted once more toward the trailer door.

I never gave another thought to anything that day. I was oblivious to any and all distractions. I left my tapes in the car. I neither saw nor even heard my brother. I was not aware of this earthly life until 8:30 that evening.

It had seemed as though I had been praying for only a short time—an hour at the most. But, it had been ten hours!

That night I packed up my Bible and books, locked up the trailer, and left. My brother Jack had apparently given up on me.

I drove out of the campground that day with an absolute surety in my soul. I knew without a *single* doubt that I had discovered the meaning of fasting and prayer.

I knew that I had experienced a personal revival in my spirit.

During the four years of Tuesdays that I fasted and prayed, my experiences were amazingly similar. I would arrive at the trailer in the morning, and I not leave until God released me. Sometimes it was six hours, sometimes twelve. It was, however, always a joy.

What did Jesus teach about fasting and prayer? He said that, "Whenever you fast, do not put on a gloomy face as the hypocrites do, for they neglect their appearance so that they will be noticed by men when they are fasting. Truly I say to you, they have their reward in full. But you, when you fast, anoint your head and wash your face so that your fasting will not be noticed by men, but by your Father who is in secret; and your Father who sees what is done in secret will reward you" (Matt. 6:16-18).

Is fasting and praying, then, something to boast about? A person could, but only if he wanted to lose his "reward." Boasting must be the farthest thing from the mind of an intercessor. Fasting and praying is certainly not something to boast about, but it is something to recommend.

Fasting and prayer is the greatest. It beats steak sandwiches, Tigers games, fishing trips, new car smells, popcorn and apples, and playing ball with my grandchildren (although this last thing ranks pretty high on my list).

Anything, in fact, that might strike me as enjoyable, exciting or exhilarating—fasting and prayer simply beats it! I would strongly recommend it.

If you are not now fasting and praying on a regular basis, you're missing a great experience.

One of the neat things about it is that you don't have to go to a trailer or a cottage to enter the presence of God. All you need is a "Do Not Disturb" sign, and a "mute" button on your telephone.

If you really stop and think about it, it just makes sense that God would not ask us to do something that did not involve joy! After all, the closer we get to Him, the closer we get to real joy!

I am convinced that the exercise of fasting and prayer, when done together (with the total exclusion of all other earthly distractions), provides the single most exhilarating experience available in this life—no exceptions!

Accept the challenge—pray for national revival, now!

History fails to record a single precedent in which nations subject to moral decay have not passed into political and economic decline. There has been a spiritual awakening to overcome the moral lapse, or a progressive deterioration leading to ultimate national disaster.

—General Douglas MacArthur, 1945 (AGCEQ).

Chapter 39—What's worse than a pit bull?

The first thing that comes to my mind, if I were to objectively answer that question, is "*two* pit bulls."

The answer I am looking for is, however, "an intercessor."

I admit this analogy might seem a bit far-fetched. But I paint such a vivid verbal picture for a reason. In my mind, an intercessor is a lot like a pit bull in at least two respects. First, much like a pit bull, an intercessor is fierce. When challenged, neither one of them will back down.

The second similarity is that they are both tenacious. Once they engage in battle, they are there to the death.

It is a simple fact, intercessors are a peculiar people. They are even quite different from other people who pray. Many people pray, many people are even "prayer warriors;" but only a few people are true intercessors.

Hannah was a true intercessor. Already approaching old age, she remained childless. For years Hannah prayed, and wept, and suffered reproach for her condition.

Yet, she would not let go of God's promise. She continued in fasting and prayer, year after year. Even though she desperately wanted to be a mother, Hannah sought only a boy child—one whom she could dedicate at birth to the work of the Lord.

God heard her plea and gave her Samuel. Hannah also kept her word, allowing Samuel to be raised in the temple. Samuel later served as priest and kingmaker.

Moses was an intercessor—he interceded for the whole nation of Israel. Moses prayed and fasted for forty days (not just once, but two times).

Jesus prayed and fasted alone in the desert for forty days.

Before Pentecost, the disciples locked themselves in the upper room. They feared for their lives—both the Jews and the Romans sought to kill them. They continued there in prayer, probably not quite certain what to expect, but definitely not willing to yield to the flesh and let go of the promise of God.

They, too, were intercessors; and their prayers were answered.

Later, in the Book of Acts, it is stated that the Apostles "were continually devoting themselves to prayer" (1:14).

Paul often fasted and prayed as well. He had little respect for those "whose god is their appetite" (Phil 3:19). Paul was an intercessor. In this he was tenacious, like a pit bull is tenacious.

Paul taught that we should "pray without ceasing" (1 Thess. 5:17). He did not mean that we should pray without a break, but that we should never give up—that we should lock on to the promises of God like a pit bull.

Cotton Mather knew what it was to be an intercessor. He locked his knuckles around the horns of the altar for four hundred ninety straight days! God responded with the revival that came to be known as the First Great Awakening.

For revival to come today, we must have intercessors. We must have continual revival prayer meetings; not just a one-week revival emphasis; not a one-day fast; not even a decade of revival prayer. We must have simple, open-ended, continual, non-sectarian, pit bull style revival prayer meetings.

Revival prayer meetings must seek the Giver more than the gift. Distractions of any sort must be rejected. Let the dead bury the dead. If an intercessor is stricken with sickness, his prayer must remain for revival over healing.

We must be willing to take God at His Word, and like Cotton Mather before us, lock on to the horns of the altar and not let go!

Not for any reason! Not until God honors His Word!

Pit bulls are the way they are by instinct—they are born that way. Intercessors, on the other hand, become intercessors only by an act of will and set purpose.

Simply stated, intercessors become intercessors only by practicing intercession, and by doing so with a vengeance!

Accept the challenge—pray for national revival, now!

If we and Our posterity
shall be true to the Christian religion,
if we and they shall live always
in the fear of God
and shall respect His Commandments,
. . . we may have the highest hopes
of the future fortunes of our country;
. . . but if we and our posterity
neglect religious instruction and authority,
violate the rules of eternal justice,
trifle with the injunctions of morality,
and recklessly destroy the political constitution
which holds us together,
no man can tell how sudden a catastrophe
may overwhelm us that shall bury
all our glory in profound obscurity.

—Daniel Webster, leading 19th century American statesman,

prominent attorney, United States Senator, and Secretary of State (AGCEQ).

Chapter 40—Organizations such as Promise Keepers, and their relationship to revival

At first I was a little angry when the national news media equated the 1990s Promise Keepers organization with the militia movement. It was a while before I began to understand how the ungodly news media could make that connection. Here's my take on this now:

I believe it is a fact that both phenomena (organizations such as Promise Keepers, and the militias) are devoted to solving the same problem: The dramatic and precipitous decline of traditional American culture. (Please understand that I do not regard any *supremacist* group as a bona fide militia.)

The militias seek national restoration through a staunch defense of the Constitution. They believe that if the Constitution is not defended, now, America will collapse. These militias are willing to use the threat of (or perhaps the actual use of) physical force to accomplish this task.

Promise Keepers, on the other hand, strives to restore traditional values through the restoration of God's ordained, primary governing unit—the family. Organizations such as Promise Keepers would point out that, according to the Bible, men are to be the priests of the household; and as such, real men must be examples of integrity. Real men must be clean (in the biblical sense).

Both groups, Promise Keepers and the militias, want to see the restoration of the great American traditional values: God, family and nation.

The ungodly news media can see this common thread running through both of these conservative groups. Further encouraging the media to make this connection is the posture the media has assumed vis-à-vis the politically conservative—that of an opposing outsider. It is often considered expedient to assemble all one's enemies under the same banner, that way one limits the war to a single front.

So, Mr. News Person, I understand how and why you equate Promise Keepers with the militias. I do not agree with you, but I understand your thinking.

Now, all that having been said, I would like to make a few comments concerning the relative merits of selected opinions put forth by the militias:

1. I agree completely with the defense of the Constitution. As far as I am concerned, the Constitution is a "Covenant Document." I, too, would defend it with my life.

2. I agree completely with the importance of traditional values.

3. I agree completely with the militias' firm stand: "This far and no more." I believe that the time has come to stand firm. Principle dictates this posture, at this time.

4. However, I believe that the militias are missing the main point. History teaches that we did not win our freedom and our nation through the brute force of military might. We did not defeat the British in a conventional manner. We were greatly out-matched, out-soldiered, out-gunned and "out-generaled."

We won our freedom because God providentially gave us victory. All the Founding Fathers recognized this fact. According to George Washington, we won our liberty on our knees. We won our liberty through revival! Even the British generals wrote in their journals about the miraculous works of God on behalf of their enemy.

French historian Alexis de Tocqueville travelled to America in 1830 to learn first hand the secret of this new nation's greatness. He wrote: "I sought for the greatness of America, not until I went to the churches of America and heard her pulpits aflame with righteousness did I understand the secret of her genius and power."

The following words are also frequently attributed to de Tocqueville, although I cannot find them in his published works: "America is great because she is good. And if America ever ceases to be good, America will cease to be great." Whether it was de Tocqueville, a contemporary, or the misappropriated notes of a later historian, it is clear what was being alluded to was America's covenant with God!

In my mind, there is no doubt that for America to be great again, it will require this nation to recognize and honor this covenant relationship with God!

I would say this to the militias: We in America do not have to use force of arms to straighten out our government. We can fire it! You will be effective only if you do the hard work of revival. Anything else is less; anything else is a cop-out; nothing else will work. America's only hope is revival!

I would say this to Promise Keeper-type organizations, now and in the future: Press on! Redouble your energies!

I would say this to CBS, NBC, ABC, CNN, and FOX News: You will probably never get it right, at least not this side of revival! I am sorry, but at this point, all of you are irrelevant! (Of course, if you wish to take part in the revival, I welcome you.)

Accept the challenge—pray for national revival, now!

Let every Student be plainly instructed, and earnestly pressed to consider well, the maine end of his life and studies is, to know God and Jesus Christ which is eternall life, John 17: 3, and therefore to lay Christ in the bottome, as the only foundation of all sound knowledge and Learning. And seeing the Lord only giveth wisedome, Let every one seriously set himself by prayer in secret to seeke it of him Prov. 2, 3.

—Original Rules and Precepts, Harvard College, Rule 2 (AGCEQ).

Chapter 41—*The monk who did not behave like a monk*

(This account was paraphrased from a book by David Bennett: *William Booth*. Minneapolis: Bethany House Publishers, Men of Faith Series (1986), pp19-22.)

It was mid-afternoon in London, and Peter had just arrived at the pub. Peter was a prizefighter, a very good prizefighter. The next day he was scheduled to tangle with a bigger man by the name of Fitzgerald.

As he stood outside the bar, a large crowd gathered around him. They wanted to see just how big he was, and how he handled himself.

Peter watched as one particularly well-dressed, handsome man made his way through the crowd. "I'm looking for work," the stranger said to the fighter.

At that, Peter started to reach into his pocket for money to help the stranger.

But, pointing to the noisy crowd of drunks gathered in anticipation of the fight, the stranger continued: "Look at those men. They are forgotten. There's my work looking for me!"

Peter, still not certain what the strange man was intending, agreed that no one really did care about those drunks, and that it would be great if someone would try to help them.

Before Peter knew what had happened, the stranger tipped his top hat and said, "I'm glad you agree. My name is William. I expect to see you and your friends tomorrow evening at my tent meeting, 7 p.m. sharp."

The stranger then turned and walked away.

The next day Peter and Fitz (short for Fitzgerald) squared off. They fought for one hour and forty-five minutes—non-stop, bare-knuckled. Both men were knocked down repeatedly. Both were cut badly. Peter's eyes were nearly swollen shut, his lips were in shreds, and the flesh on both of his hands was laid back to the bone.

Finally, Fitz could fight no more. Even though he was the bigger and better-known of the two, he had to concede.

After Peter accepted the customary accolades (and, of course, his pay for the fight), he then rushed off to get cleaned up for the preacher's meeting.

As he walked into the tent, he was greatly distressed by the jeers and hoots of the crowd. While William was doing his best to make himself heard above the shouting, he was not able to handle the crowd.

Quietly, Peter walked up on the platform with William. He took off his coat, baring his huge, hairy chest, and just stood there motionless.

Immediately the crowd became totally silent, allowing William to finish his sermon without another interruption.

"How did you do that?" William asked Peter afterwards.

Spreading his swollen lips into a wide toothless grin, Peter explained: "My name is Peter Monk. I am a prizefighter. And people respect prize-fighters; especially Irish prizefighters who win!"

The preacher responded, "My name is William Booth. And you're not a happy man, Peter Monk! You'll perish like a dog! You're living for the devil and the devil will have you!"

Placing his hand on Monk's shoulder, Booth said: "Peter Monk, I will make a man out of you yet!"

By the end of the week Peter Monk was born again, and was working for Booth as manager of the East London Soup Kitchen. This type of conversion was repeated millions of times, around the world, as William Booth's Salvation Army waged its guerrilla warfare against the strongholds of Satan. The year was 1865—it was a period of great revival.

Accept the challenge—pray for national revival, now!

Chapter 42—*Bertha, won't you please come home?*

At the time of the original writing of this chapter, Bertha had become legally blind, but she could still see a little bit, out of one eye.

To the casual observer, that would suggest it was time for Bertha to trade her Chevy in for a burro.

That shouldn't be a problem for Bertha, though, since she lived in the back hills of Mexico. A burro actually makes more sense than a Chevy in that terrain.

Bertha didn't talk about it much, but I think she was pushing ninety when I first encountered her. I really didn't know exactly how old she was, nor did I care. I was, however, aware that she had long ago lost her official financial support for her missionary work—because of her age.

But Bertha's frailty never slowed her down. Through the financial support of friends and individual churches, Bertha quietly just kept on winning souls.

She did return to the States some years ago, to spend a short time with her terminally-ill sister. Soon after the funeral, however, Bertha was on her way back to her beloved Mexico.

I'll bet she took comfort reading about another great missionary—Paul. He, too, would have been considered "legally blind." Paul wrote, "I have learned to be content in whatever circumstances I am" (Phil. 4:11). Bertha possessed the same rugged determination as did Paul. I doubt that either one of them ever spent much time feeling sorry for themselves.

Despite his "handicap," Paul's work triggered the greatest revival in the history of the world. In fact, his work will always serve as the standard for Christian evangelism.

Bertha's work, along with her missionary brothers and sisters, also produced a monumental revival (you can read about this more in Chapter 3). There are now more born-again Christians than ever before in the history of the world.

Humble missionaries in Mainland China, doing work similar to that of Bertha in Mexico, have reputedly produced two hundred million born-again Christians. In that Asian land, the missionaries toiled under the constant threat of death.

Amazing missionary work is ongoing in Eastern Europe, Korea and South America. Whole nations in Central and South America are turning to God. It has even been jokingly suggested that if the revival in Brazil continues at its present rate, within a few years everyone in that nation will be a professing Christian!

America, on the other hand, has so far missed out on this revival. While millions around the world are literally climbing over church pews to get to the altars, most American churchgoers are checking their watches.

Unlike Bertha and Paul, many of our big-time evangelists are more interested in how their hair looks on television than they are in the condition of our national soul.

Friends, this nation is going to hell at breakneck speed—our schools are a battlefield, our courts a joke, and our young people have no sense of direction. Yet, our so-called spiritual leaders continue to strut around like roosters, telling us that "as Christians, we have a right to be rich."

Please, Bertha, come home. We, in America, need you. We need you to teach us the true meaning of 2 Chronicles 7:14. (Shortly after this writing, Bertha left Mexico for good. She went to her "real" home.)

Accept Bertha's challenge—pray for national revival, now!

Chapter 43—Is God saving His best for last?

I recently heard it said (again) that "God is saving His best revival for America!"

This idea is based on the belief that because America has been instrumental in spreading revival fires around the world, God is therefore saving the best revival of all for us here in America (something like a reward).

Well, try as I might, I could not think of a single Scripture, or an historical event, that would support the notion that revival has ever come about as the result of good works.

Simply stated—revival is *never* given as a reward for anything. My studies indicate that revival comes to a people only when that people, as an act of will, return to God. Never does revival come as a reward for good works! Revival comes to the Church only as the result of hungry, humble people seeking Him.

If, then, revival in America is not to be expected as the result of our past good works, no matter how noble they might have been, how then will revival come to pass in this country?

Revival will come to America when America repents—revival always demands repentance.

Not only am I totally convinced that America will have a great revival, I am equally certain that this revival will not come because the Church in America has somehow *deserved* it. Not in any sense.

The real question is not, "is God saving his best for America?" The right question to be asked is this: "What it is going to take to bring this nation to repentance?" I believe America will repent either because it wants to repent, or because it has been brought to its knees against its will, kicking and screaming. Right now, I think the latter is more likely.

Not that I would like to see calamity, but I think the elitist pride in this nation (both inside and outside the Church) virtually dictates God's judgment. Things could change overnight; but as it stands right now, I see major troubles on the horizon.

However, my seemingly pessimistic view of the situation is actually anything *but* pessimistic. In fact, I see nothing at all to suggest that revival and judgment are mutually exclusive. According to 2 Chronicles 7:13-14, the two actually bear a causal type of relationship—judgment can lead to repentance, which is necessary for revival.

As I have stated numerous times in *Wind*—I am *totally* convinced America will eventually have revival, but first it must determine the shortest distance between its face and the floor, and bring the two together.

I have heard many Christian leaders state that they sense something cataclysmic is about to occur in this nation—perhaps a national calamity, or some other event of unprecedented magnitude. I sense the same thing. If the Church in America persists in its arrogance, I would not even be surprised to see this nation crumble—perhaps quickly.

So, *is* God saving His best for last?

No!

If anything, God is mercifully holding back His hand of judgment, for a time, giving us one last chance to repent on our own.

Our challenge is to lay our faces on the floor, daily, and plead for the mercy of God over this land. And to do it quickly.

Accept the challenge—pray for national revival, now!

Chapter 44—Why did I write this book in the first place?

That's a fair question: Why is there a *Wind*? The answer is simple. In the summer of 1993 I sensed that God was *calling* me to intercede for national revival.

It was not as though I suddenly decided that I should engage myself in this project. As I discussed in the "Introduction," I already had all the work I could handle, and I certainly could not afford to take time off work. But I became convinced that it was an effort that must be made, and that I was one of those who must make it. These are the events that preceded my involvement, as I remember them:

It was a little after 9 p.m. on a hot July night. It was a Friday. I had just finished putting on a demonstration of a residential electronic security system at the home of a potential customer. As I started my car, I remembered that the Detroit Tigers were playing. When I reached down to tune in the game, the Holy Spirit stopped me. I am not suggesting that someone or something *physically* grabbed my arm, and stopped me from changing the radio station. I am saying that the Holy Spirit impressed my mind to leave the radio alone. Charles Stanley was teaching, and I sensed strongly that his message was for me.

However, being a huge Tigers fan, I reached down a second time to tune in the game. And again the Holy Spirit stopped me. I heard no audible voice, and there were no bolts of lightning. I simply felt constrained to listen to what Charles Stanley had to say.

At that point I decided I could live without my Tigers game.

The teaching was on obedience. The gist of the message was that our whole Christian experience, and the effectiveness of our witness, hinged on our total submission and obedience to the will of God.

The Holy Spirit made it crystal clear to me. I felt a lot like I did on the night I got saved. It was as though electricity was pulsing throughout my body. As the message neared completion, I sensed a wave of self-righteous pride flow through me. I thought: "God wanted to see if I would obey Him, and I did. So, I guess it means I passed that test."

I pulled my car into a parking place, so I could listen carefully to the remainder of Charles Stanley's message. It was powerful. It convicted me. I kept repeating "surrender and obedience" in my mind.

It was then that something very strange happened. Just as Rev. Stanley broke away from his message for a few promotional words about his ministry, my radio changed stations—*all by itself*. It switched over to the Tigers game just as the last out was made. The announcer declared the game over, gave the score, and named the winning pitcher. I was shocked.

Then, just as quickly, it switched back for Charles Stanley's closing comments on surrender and obedience. I had not touched the radio! I had chills all over my body.

I realized that there could be a natural explanation for a phenomenon such as this. I remembered from my classes at DeVry Technical Institute that the most logical explanation might be "harmonics." However, the radio had a digital tuner, and it was new. I had just purchased the car—a Lincoln Town Car, Signature Series. It was not a cheap radio. The frequency of Charles Stanley was 1480, and the Tigers game was on 1240 or 1300. From what I knew about harmonics, these frequencies should not readily "harmonize." The numbers on the digital radio did not change.

Nothing like that had ever happened to me before, nor has it ever occurred after. I still see no other explanation for this except that is was God trying to get my attention.

I hurried home. I gathered my whole family together in our standard meeting place (in front of the fireplace in the basement), and announced what God had done that night. I told them the whole story.

My conclusion (at that time) was that God wanted His people to surrender and obey Him, and because I was faithful in this instance, by *not* changing the radio station to my ball game, God was pleased with me, and He was going to bless me. We prayed, had devotions, and we all went off to bed. My pride was bubbling over.

However, my euphoria was short lived. At about 5 a.m. the following morning, as I started to awake out of a deep sleep, I sensed that God was speaking to my heart again—this time in a dream. He impressed on my spirit in that dream that I had wrongly interpreted His work the night before. He was in no way rewarding me for my good works. Rather, He was awakening my spirit to pray for revival. He revealed to me that I must seek revival with all of my heart, without ceasing, *for* a season. I did not understand the "for a season" part, but I accepted it by faith.

Again, there was no audible voice. This was a dream.

I realized then that what God was impressing on me was going to be much more involved than simply *not* tuning in to a Tigers game.

As I lie there silently in bed, still not fully awake, He further spoke to me again by dream that within a short time the reality of this revelation would be confirmed by two witnesses. I then stirred and became fully awake. Nothing like this had ever happened to me before. I was frightened.

I really did not know exactly what God was commanding me to do. But, at 6 a.m. on that Saturday morning, I got my entire family up (cruel and unusual?), and again we all went down to our little meeting place in front of the fireplace. There I told them exactly what I felt God had revealed to me—that I must seek His face for revival with all my heart.

I explained that God was not rewarding me by providing a box score, but that He was telling me I must obey Him by seeking revival. And that

He would reward that effort—not with personal gain, but with national revival. I told them that God would confirm this message to me through two witnesses. I also told them at that time that this would not be a permanent occupation. That God had given this job to me to do for a season. I had no notion what I was to do, or for how long, but I figured that God would show me what to do, and that He would let me know when my part of it was finished.

I recognized the fact that I was totally ignorant about revival. So, later that day I went to the area Christian bookstores and bought a number of books on revival: two by L. Ravenhill, and a couple on the life of Charles Finney, the Wesley brothers, and some others. I read all day.

From what I learned about previous revivals, I determined that God wanted me to fast and pray when I interceded for revival. So, I talked it over with my wife, and we decided that I would and spend Tuesdays in fasting and prayer. (As I wrote earlier, I initially tried staying at home when I fasted, but it did not work. So, after a couple weeks, I decided to go off to Fa-Ho-Lo (a Christian campground near Jackson, Michigan) on my Tuesday fast days. We owned a mobile home there.)

Immediately after my first Tuesday fast day (before I left for home), I wrote down my thoughts regarding national revival.

The next day I read what I had written. I thought it was powerful, and that I should do something with it.

I typed it up and sent it out to some pastors and publications. I continued doing that every week. I called my little newsletter *The New Revivalist*. I took the name from a publication that emerged from the Pentecostal Revival at the beginning of the twentieth century. Frank Bartleman, the man who chronicled the move of God at Azusa Street, had published a newsletter he called *The Revivalist*.

Immediately two different small newspapers picked it up and began running my articles under the heading "Wind of Revival." For over four years I wrote and published those articles—about two hundred in total.

Remember, in my dream God had told me that the validity of this message would be born out by two witnesses? Well, about six months into my fasting and prayer, the salesman from one of the publications that carried my writings approached me with some information. He told me that he had received several calls from a man he had known for years, and that the man wanted to talk to me.

Earlier I had told my friend that I would not talk to anyone about this. I simply had no interest in what anyone else had to say. I wished to hear only from God, and I was not about to allow anyone to interject spurious thoughts into what I felt God was telling me. Jeff and I had talked about that several times before. Many people wanted to discuss revival with me. I thought that Jeff knew better than to even suggest this to me.

Jeff, this time, was *very* persistent. He said, "This is different. I think you need to talk to this guy. I know him to be a real gentleman, and he *really* wants to talk to you."

Just to make Jeff happy, I agreed to have a cup of coffee with his friend.

We met in the evening at a local restaurant. I had never met him before, so I did not know what to expect. We had agreed over the phone that I would recognize him because he would have a copy of my column setting on the table. I walked in the restaurant, and began looking for the paper. I found it at a table where *two* men were sitting (I had expected only one). I introduced myself, and sat down. After a short time of small talk, the younger of the two asked me this question: "Think back. Do you recall the *exact* date that God revealed Himself to you with regard to revival? And what the circumstances were?"

I didn't have to think about it. I knew the exact date and time, and I told them.

The two of them just looked at each other for a long moment. Then the older one looked back at me, and with tears in his eyes, he started to talk. He said that the two of them were at a prayer meeting in Toronto that very night, at that very time. First one of them stood to give a prophecy on national revival for America, and then the other did the same. They were not sitting together. They had never met before, they had simply heard the other's prophecy from opposite sides of the auditorium. Yet, both prophetic messages were virtually the same.

After the meeting, they looked each other up. They were amazed to discover that they were both from Grand Rapids (Michigan), which was my hometown as well.

My revelation had come that same night. And, as nearly as we could tell, at *exactly* the same time. I recognized immediately that these two gentlemen were the witnesses that God had promised to send me.

Now, you must understand, during all the years that I fasted and prayed for revival, writing and publishing articles every week, not once had I ever published the story about that night with Charles Stanley and the Detroit Tigers. Not only had I not published it, I had not even told my close friends. I put it in writing one time, in the form of a private letter to my pastor. But that was it. The publishers of the newspapers that carried my column were not even aware of the details.

These two men had never heard it before, nor had they read it. They were just following God's command. They commented that they were not even sure why they had felt the need to look me up, except that they were also seeking a confirmation for their prophecy. I never talked to them again.

Well, as I said, for about four years God held my hand as I fasted and prayed for revival in America. He gave me a clear mind as I wrote and published. All the time I knew that at some point He would take this part of the burden from me. I knew that I was not to go into the ministry. I had a business to run. I had over twenty employees, most of whom had families that, to one degree or another, also relied on my business remaining profitable. I had major responsibilities.

Several times I talked to my wife about this. I would say that I really did not know how God was going to end my role in this, but that I knew it was not a forever thing for me. I strongly believed that once started, the revival would move into the churches, and would there be propagated by those called by God into the ministry. I really had no notion of what He would do when He was finished with me on this project, I just knew that my involvement was "for a season."

One morning about four years later I found out.

As I awoke that day, I discovered that my right hand had swollen to the point that I could not close it. Not only was I unable to use a computer, I was barely able to drive a car. I had to carry pliers in order to turn the ignition on and off. It hurt so badly that I was forced to keep my hand propped up on the headrest of the passenger seat when I went on sales appointments.

The pain was so intense I could not drive the one and one-half hours to Jackson, much less write and publish articles. This condition persisted for a month. I still fasted and prayed, at home, but I could no longer travel and write.

Then God spoke to me again in a dream, telling me that I was finished with this part of the job.

I told my wife that I had heard from God again, and that I was finished publishing about revival. My hand then healed within a week. I have never had a problem with it again.

As it turned out, I was almost right. While God had taken the burden of *writing* on revival away from me, it became clear that He was not entirely absolving me of responsibility. In the winter of 2000, God began stirring my heart to publish these articles (at least as many of them as I could retrieve) on the web. I did not want to do this. I really was quite pleased to think that He had released me from this obligation altogether.

Over the course of several months I repeatedly rejected His leading on this issue. I kept telling myself that it was actually my flesh crying out for attention; that, if I published the revival articles on the web, I would be doing so for personal recognition.

However, because I did have several other web sites, I knew it would not be a huge task for me to create another one. So, in June of 2000 I registered www.newrevivalist.com, and posted about one hundred revival articles on that site.

One of the most interesting things about this stage of the project is that had I not revisited these articles after initially publishing them, and had I not converted them to something other than a DOS-based program, they might all have been lost forever.

Even in 2000 I found that many of the floppy discs had been damaged or were otherwise unusable. In many instances I actually had to scan the articles from my old *New Revivalist* newsletter. (The web site, www. newrevivalist.com, now serves to introduce *Wind*.)

I still, however, have not explained why at this time I am publishing *Wind*. The truth is that I was content leaving the revival articles on the *New Revivalist* web site. There they could be accessed easily by anyone Googling "revival." That seemed like the right thing to do, at that time.

Then, three years ago, my wife and I began writing a six-volume set of books on "comparative mnemonics." As we were preparing to publish the first volume of the series, my spirit was again stirred with regard to the revival series.

"How," I thought, "can I publish these other works, and ignore the articles on revival?"

I then began to understand what God meant when He told me in the dream that I must seek revival "without ceasing, for a season." Up to that point, I was conflicted about the nature and tenure of my role. It became clear that I had to publish the revival articles again, this time in a book.

So, I talked it over with Evie, and we determined that the right thing to do was to publish *Wind* first. We held back the series on comparative mnemonics, and concentrated time and resources on *Wind*.

That's why the little book you are now reading exists.

If God impresses you to intercede for national revival, I know *Wind* will be helpful to you.

It is my hope and prayer that God will touch your heart, and convict you (as He did me) of the need for powerful intercessory prayer. That's what it will take for revival.

Accept the challenge—pray for national revival, now!

Author's Notes: It might seem a little strange to find this chapter positioned so deeply into this book. It does, after all, provide what would seem to be "introductory material." There is a reason for my not including it closer to the front. When I read this chapter objectively, it gives me the sense that it could be interpreted as something an author might *create* to add credibility to his book. I held it back to the latter chapters because I am fairly certain anyone who has made it this deeply into *Wind* has most likely caught the vision for revival; that he sees and understands what I am writing about; and that he is ready to do his part. If that is you, then reading this chapter might be giving you Holy Spirit conviction, just as it does to me every time I read it.

*We have staked the whole future of
American civilization,
not upon the power of government,
far from it.
We have staked the future
of all of our political institutions
upon the capacity of mankind for self-government;
upon the capacity of each and all of us
to govern ourselves
according to the Ten Commandments of God.*

—James Madison, Fourth President of the

United States

and "Chief Architect of the Constitution" (AGCEQ).

Chapter 45—Who will it be?

I realize that I have discussed numerous times throughout the pages of this book the fact that I am convinced that the Third Great Awakening has already begun, and it is alive and well in America today. I realize that I have probably belabored that notion. Nevertheless, I feel the need (or desire) to address it once more from a slightly different angle.

The biggest question mark that I see, with regard to this new national revival, has to do with the nature of those who will provide God with the best conduit for it. That is, who will be the person, or group of people, used by God to facilitate this revival?

In the past, the most effective revivalists generally were not great orators. Typically they did not want to lead anything. They just couldn't help themselves. That was the case with Charles Finney, and many others. Some of them were downright scoundrels.

I wonder if this revival might find its fertile ground on one or more college campuses, or in the nation's prisons. I would not be shocked if groups of inmates banded together to seek God's face for national revival. After all, was not the Apostle Paul in prison when God used his hand to write some of the most stirring narratives recorded in the New Testament? Perhaps it will be soldiers in the military who will seek God's face for revival—that's what happened among those serving in the Confederate Army during the Civil War.

It is possible that it will be a prominent person in the Church, such as a David Wilkerson (author of *The Cross and the Switchblade*, and numerous other books). In my opinion, this man is a modern-day prophet.

However, basing my *guess* on past revivals, it is quite possible (if not likely) that the mantle of leadership for this revival will not rest on the shoulders of current religious leaders. Perhaps there will not even be a single figure, such as a Charles Finney, who will rise to prominence. I would not be surprised if this awakening was totally God-centric; so that no one person would stand out to take credit. Ideally, in my mind, that is how it should be.

In fact, as I suggest frequently in this book, I believe God is looking for average people—those who are willing to shed pride and arrogance; who will fast and pray with utter abandon; and who will truly seek His face.

Who knows what group of people (or individuals) will be willing to step up and pay that price? What if, this time, the revival fields bloom in the prayer closets of moms?

Or in the bedrooms of children?

Or on the field of battle?

Or in the boardrooms of corporations?

Or in the offices of lawyers?

Or in the classrooms of interceding students?

Or in the many prison cells across our great land?

Or, perhaps, in *your* prayer closet?

I'm glad I'm not God. He already knows how it's going to happen. I only get to watch in wonderment and expectation.

Accept the challenge—pray for national revival, now!

Chapter 46—National revival, now!

The thing that is hardest for me to understand is why good, thinking people would disregard such a simple, yet time-proven solution—national restoration follows revival, which is brought about by 2 Chronicles 7:14 praying.

For decades this country has been sliding into a hole. We have sunk so deeply into that abyss that many (if not most) of the thinkers of the world have already written us off as a world power. Others have gone so far as to suggest that the U.S. may itself be slipping into some form of fascism, perhaps not unlike that of Nazi Germany. Strangely, some writers seem almost gleeful about our impending demise.

I wonder how many of them have taken the time to realize just what that will mean (if the United States ceases to be the world leader). Are they aware that for the past century it has been the U.S. that has provided a safety net for all the world's peoples? Sure, the U.S. has been a highly imperfect leader (even selfish at times), but were it not for U.S. strength and resolve, the despots of the world would be ruling right now (then welcome to the New Dark Age).

It was the U.S. that turned the tables in World Wars I and II, then financed the rebuilding and re-tooling of its defeated enemies. It was the U.S. that blocked the Soviet Union from world domination. And, it is on the strength of the U.S. that the peoples of all the NATO nations currently depend for stability and protection—hundreds of millions of people. If these thinkers and political leaders are correct in their assessment, and the U.S. does continue to slip into oblivion, the next Hitler or Stalin will have carte blanche at conquering the world.

Even the oil producers of the Near East need the U.S. to preserve their stability. Without a strong and vibrant U.S., it will not be a matter of whether their oil is purchased with dollars, rubles, yen, euros, or some other form of currency. It just simply won't be purchased at all—it will be free to the conqueror.

Think about a world without the U.S. If you're good with serfdom, followed by (or perhaps *preceded* by) nuclear war, then you definitely should disregard this little book.

If, however, you've grown fond of freedom and liberty (and they are not the same), then heed the call of *Wind*.

Keep in mind, of course, that it took generations to get to our current condition—restoration will not be overnight. But it is a fact—the sooner we get started doing the hard work of revival, the sooner healing can and will take place.

Finally, I have frequently been asked this question: "Who has a right to seek revival?" The answer to that is simple as well: If you consider 2 Chronicles 7:13-14 to be God's Word (and applicable today), then you are included.

Simply read and do: "If . . . My people who are called by My name humble themselves and pray and seek My face and turn from their wicked ways, then I will hear from heaven, and will forgive their sin and will heal their land" (2 Chronicles 7:13-14).

What are you waiting for?

Conclusion

My children are always very thoughtful. Before they buy a gift for Evie or me, they think it through first. I can picture them debating at length as to what would be the perfect thing to buy for us on every gift-giving occasions.

This past spring, I think for my birthday, they bought me two tickets to Brooklyn International Speedway to watch Johnny Benson race in the NASCAR Truck Series.

That was a perfect gift for me for a number of reasons. There were two tickets, so Evie could go with me. Johnny Benson lives in the Grand Rapids area, and is a fan favorite at the local small-venue racing circuits (you could say that I am a Johnny Benson fan). And, like Johnny Benson, I am a Chevrolet Camaro aficionado. I currently own two of the wonderful machines, one of which reputedly was JB's personal demo car from a local dealership. That may or may not be true, but I like to think it is. Needless to say, I was pleased with the tickets.

Unfortunately, when we arrived at Brooklyn on race day, we learned that Johnny Benson had been seriously injured the day before in a sprint car crash at a Grand Rapids track. Evie and I still enjoyed the race, took lots of photographs, and wished Johnny Benson a speedy recovery. It was a great day.

It was, however, the drive back to Grand Rapids that provided the most wrenching emotional experience of the day. Because the Brooklyn Raceway is located near Fa-Ho-Lo (the campground where I had gone for fasting and praying), Evie and I thought it would be interesting to take a drive through it. We had not visited the area for the past twelve years. We did not know what to expect.

As we entered the long drive that led into the heart of the facility, we were drawn back to the times when we would come as a family to spend a week each summer. Evie and the children never joined me for Tuesdays' fasting and prayer during those four years, but for many years we did spend our summer vacations at the campground.

As we drove through the winding roads, we were very impressed with all the improvements. There were several very impressive new buildings on the campus, including a magnificent recently-completed chapel. The grounds were spotless, and everyone we approached greeted us with a warm smile.

The trailer that we owned during the 1980s and 90s was not located in the part of the facility that had been renovated. In fact, we were amazed to see that virtually every one of the trailers that were parked along our remote little road were still there. Nothing much had changed over the past twelve years in that part of the campus, except all those trailers looked a little older.

When we approached the trailer that had belonged to us, we were doubly gripped. We pulled up in front of it, and stopped. Neither of us could say a word. Tears welled up in our eyes as we just stared at it. Both Evie and I could still sense the power of God emanating from its walls.

The trailer was not new when we bought it. Earlier it had served as the summer home and prayer closet for the Reverend Thomas Trask, who for years served as General Superintendant of the Assemblies of God.

While we could not be certain, it appeared to Evie and me as though it had not been occupied since we sold it. It was intact, with no broken windows, but branches had fallen all around it, and they remained where they had fallen. I recall thinking, as we waited there, "All this place needs is a rake, a pail of soapy water, a vacuum cleaner, and a bucket of intercessory tears." It was as though the trailer was crying out for attention.

In a very real sense, that is exactly what America is doing right now—it is crying out for our attention, and for revival tears.

It is clear that the glory of God has been forced out of our nation. The Spirit of God that won the battles during the Revolutionary War; that freed this nation from the yoke of slavery (our greatest national sin); that provided the moral resolve to conquer the tyrants of World War I and World War II; and that gave us the power to provide freedom for much of the rest of the world in the past century; the glory of *His* Spirit has departed from America.

Unless we resolve to bring it back, America will cease to exist as a viable entity in this dangerous world. That will create a power vacuum not experienced since the fall of Rome. Anyone who has studied history knows what the Dark Ages were all about.

God told us what to do to get His glory back. We still have a choice. He gave us this clear directive: "If I shut up the heavens so that there is no rain, or if I command the locust to devour the land, or if I send pestilence among My people, and My people who are called by my name humble themselves and pray and seek my face and turn from their wicked ways, then will I hear from heaven, will forgive their sin and will heal their land" (2 Chron. 7:13-14).

It all depends on whether or not we care enough about our country, our own souls, and the future of our children, to implement it.

It is totally up to you, and me. God did His part, will you do yours?

(Regarding Slavery)
It is a great national sin.
It is a sin of the Church.
The Churches, by their silence,
and by permitting slaveholders
to belong to their communion,
have been consenting to it. . . .
Let Christians of all denominations meekly,
but firmly, come forth, and pronounce their verdict;
then wash their hands of this thing; let them give forth and write
on the head and front of this great abomination,
"SIN."

—Charles Grandison Finney, Lectures on Revival.

Afterword

Earlier in this book I stated that if it appeared the interest existed, I would publish a second (and possibly a third) Volume of *Wind*. If that turns out to be the case, the next *Wind* will start out with a multipart segment on revival's historical role in the abolition of slavery (which I regard as our nation's greatest corporate sin).

When I first published an article on this topic, I was immediately confronted by a very articulate African-American gentleman who took exception to that notion. Generally, I did not respond to critics. However, in his case, I felt I had to.

The gentleman wrote two letters, and both were passionate and polite. While I never had the opportunity to meet the man, I did get to know and appreciate him through his correspondence.

I will never forget the day that the managing editor of one of the newspapers that ran my articles called me about this matter. He said, "Mike, I need to have you read something. Are you going to be in your office for the next ten minutes?"

A few minutes later he and his wife drove up. I did not have much time (because I was on my way to a sales appointment), so I met them in the parking lot. He handed me a two-page letter.

"You have a critic," he said. "I would like you to respond to him."

I asked the editor if he was familiar with the writer, and he indicated that "he was a very respected member of the African-American community. His comments *must* be addressed."

If there is a volume 2 of *Wind*, I'm sure you will find that the letter writer's comments were thought out, and that his points were well made.

I did, however, feel at the time (and still do) that revival movements played a large part in ending slavery in America, not propagating it. I believe I demonstrate that point very well in my responses.

My hope and prayer today is that the Third Great Awakening can remove even residual racism from America.

How to buy and use this book

This book can be purchased directly through Amazon. Simply go to http://www.amazon.com, and search for "*Wind*, by Mike Carrier." Buy a few copies (they make great gifts, especially for Christmas), and current Amazon policy will ship them free when you order in quantity (be sure to check with Amazon to verify the status of this policy, as it is subject to change).

Parents and grandparents, you should buy a copy of *Wind* for each member of your family who is high school or college age. It can change lives.

You can also go to your favorite bookstore. If you don't find it on the shelf, you can request that it be ordered for you.

Once you have *Wind* in your hand, don't let go of it. Just because you have read it once, go back to it often. Each time you do, God will find something new in it just for you. There are pages at the back for you to record what God is speaking to your heart.

Use *Wind* (along with your Bible) in your personal devotions, when you lead your youth group, and in your prayer meetings.

Email all your friends and tell them to buy it. Put it on your Facebook. Twitter it. The more people reading and following *Wind*, the sooner we can have national revival.

Wind is the clarion call you have been waiting for. Heed that call, and help usher in the Third Great Awakening.

Selected reading

W hen I first entered into my period of fasting and prayer for national revival, I went out and bought a number of books, and kept them at the trailer where I prayed. I found those books to be very helpful, so I am providing a list of them for you to consider.

Some of the books have revival as their subject, while others are on various related topics.

I have in my personal library over one thousand books and other publications dating from 1806 to the end of that century. That means they would encompass the last years of the First Great Awakening, and most of the Second. You will find that I quoted from some of them in the pages of *Wind*. I do not include them in this list, as it would be virtually impossible for you to find them.

In the case of some of the books listed, I was unable to buy them at my local store (remember, I originally wrote these articles during the pre-Amazon era); so I found them at public and university libraries. I think there were only a half dozen of the books that were out of print.

I strongly recommend that you pull all of these books off the shelves of your public or university libraries. If they look like they might be helpful to you, check them out, or better yet buy them.

Not included on this list are any books written over the past fifteen years, as they were not available to me in the 1990s.

Bartleman, Frank. *Azusa Street*. Plainfield, NJ: Logos
        International (1980).
Bennett, David M. *D.L Moody*. Minneapolis: Bethany House
        Publishers, Men of Faith Series (1989).

_____. *William Booth.* Minneapolis: Bethany House Publishers, Men of Faith Series (1986).

Booker, Richard. *How to Prepare for the Coming Revival.* Shippensburg, PA: Destiny Image Publishers (1982).

_____. *Supernatural Prayer and Fasting—The Keys to Triumphant Living.* Shippensburg, PA: Destiny Image Publishers (1993).

Bradford, M.E. *A Worthy Company—Brief lives of the Framers of the United States Constitution.* Marlborough, NH: Plymouth Rock Foundation, Inc. (1982).

Dallimore, Arnold A. *A Heart Set Free—The Life of Charles Wesley.* Westchester, Illinois: Crossway Books (1988).

DeTocqueville, Alexis. *Democracy in America* (translated by George Lawrence, edited by J.P. Mayer). New York: Harper Collins (1969).

Dorsett, Lyle Wesley. *E.M. Bounds, Man of Prayer.* Grand Rapids: Zondervan Publishing House (1991).

Drummond, Lewis. *Eight Keys to Biblical Revival.* Minneapolis: Bethany House Publishers (1994).

Dupuis, Richard A. G. and Rosell, Garth M., editors. *The Memoirs of Charles G. Finney.* Grand Rapids: Zondervan Publishing House (1989).

Edwards, Brian H. *Revival, A People Saturated with God.* Durham, England: Evangelical Press (1990).

Federer, William J. *America's God and Country Encyclopedia of Quotations.* Coppell, Texas: Fame Publishing, Inc. (1994).

Hardman, Keith J. *Charles Grandison Finney 1792-1875, Revivalist and Reformer.* Grand Rapids: Baker Book House Company (1990).

Hawking, Stephen W. *A Brief History of Time.* New York: Bantam Books (1988).

Hywel-Davies, Jack. *The Life of Smith Wigglesworth—One Man, One Holy Passion.* Ann Arbor: Servant Publications (1987).

Johnson, Kevin, ed. *Charles G. Finney Lectures on Revival.* Minneapolis: Bethany House Publishers (1988).

Kauffman, Stuart A. *The Origins of Order.* New York: Oxford University Press (1993).

Lederman, Leon. *The God Particle.* New York: Bantam Doubleday Dell Publishing Group, Inc. (1993).

Lutz, Donald S. and Hyneman, Charles S. *American Political Writing During the Founding Era—1760-1805, Volume 1.* Indianapolis: Liberty Press (1983).

Parkhurst, Louis Gifford Jr., editor and compiler. *Principles of Revival, Charles G. Finney.* Minneapolis: Bethany House Publishers (1987).

Pratney, Winkie A. *Revival—Principles to Change the World.* Springdale, PA: Whitaker House (1983).

Ravenhill, Leonard, ed. *The Best of E.M. Bounds in a Single Volume.* Minneapolis: Bethany House Publishers (1961).

_____. *Meat for Men.* Minneapolis: Bethany House Publishers (1961).

_____. *Revival God's Way.* Minneapolis: Bethany House Publishers (1983).

_____. *Revival Praying.* Minneapolis: Bethany House Publishers (1962).

_____. *Why Revival Tarries.* Minneapolis: Bethany House Publishers (1959).

Smoot, George and Davidson, Keay. *Wrinkles in Time.* New York: Avon Books (1993).

Taylor, J. Hudson. *Hudson Taylor.* Minneapolis: Bethany House Publishers, Men of Faith Series (No date given).

Tipler, Frank J. *The Physics of Immortality*. New York: Doubleday (1994).

Tracy, Joseph. *The Great Awakening—A History of the Revival of Religion in the time of Edwards and Whitefield*. Edinburgh: The Banner of Truth Trust (First published in 1842, Reprinted in 1976, and 1989).

Weakley, Clare George Jr., ed. *The Nature of Revival—John Wesley, Charles Wesley and George Whitefield*. Minneapolis: Bethany House Publishers (1987).

Whitefield, George. *George Whitefield's Journals*. Edinburgh: The Banner of Truth Trust (First published 1738-1741, Reprinted in 1992).

May God Bless you
As you heed this call for Revival

Mike

Proof

Made in the USA
Charleston, SC
03 December 2009